Project
Management

Phil Baguley

TEACH YOURSELF BOOKS

For UK orders: please contact Bookpoint Ltd, 39 Milton Park, Abingdon, Oxon OX14 4TD. Telephone: (44) 01235 400414, Fax: (44) 01235 400454. Lines are open from 9.00–6.00, Monday to Saturday, with a 24 hour message answering service. Email address: orders@bookpoint.co.uk

For USA & Canada orders: please contact NTC/Contemporary Publishing, 4255 West Touhy Avenue, Lincolnwood, Illinois 60646–1975, USA. Telephone: (847) 679 5500, Fax (847) 679 2494.

Long renowned as the authoritative source for self-guided learning – with more than 30 million copies sold worldwide – the *Teach Yourself* series includes over 200 titles in the fields of languages, crafts, hobbies, business and education.

A catalogue entry for this title is available from The British Library.

Library of Congress Catalog Card Number: On file

First published in UK 1999 by Hodder Headline Plc, 338 Euston Road, London, NW1 3B

First published in US 1999 by NTC/Contemporary Publishing, 4255 West Touhy Avenue, Lincolnwood (Chicago), Illinois 60646–1975 USA.

The 'Teach Yourself' name and logo are registered trade marks of Hodder & Stoughton Lt

Typeset by Transet Limited, Coventry, England.
Printed in Great Britain for Hodder & Stoughton Educational, a division of Hodder Headline Plc, 338 Euston Road, London NW1 3BH by Cox & Wyman Ltd, Reading, Berkshire.

Impression number   10 9 8 7 6 5 4
Year   2004 2003 2002 2001 2000

CONTENTS

Introduction _____ **1**

1 **Projects, projects and projects** _____ **3**
Projects old and new _____ 3
Projects now _____ 4
How and why _____ 4
Big or small _____ 6
Concrete or ideas _____ 7
Work and play _____ 7
The Five Fundamentals _____ 8
Definitions _____ 10
The project boundaries _____ 11
The project life cycle _____ 13
Project priorities _____ 15
Projects and people _____ 15
Summary _____ 16

2 **Which project?** _____ **17**
Choice _____ 17
Uncertainty and risk _____ 18
Identify the risk _____ 19
Reducing the risk _____ 20
Yes or No _____ 22
Choosing _____ 22
Choosing without numbers _____ 23
Choosing by numbers _____ 26
Summary _____ 29

3 **Your project organization** _____ **30**
Organizing _____ 30
Organizations _____ 31
Structures, leaders and people _____ 32

Projects and organizations – the differences _____ 33
What sort of project organization? _____ 34
Project aspects _____ 35
Project organizations _____ 36
    The Integrated project organization _____ 36
    The Stand Alone project organization _____ 37
    The Matrix project organization_____ 38
Your project organization_____ 39
Project procedures and specifications _____ 41
Summary _____ 45

4 Plans for your project_____ 46
Planning – now or never _____ 46
Projects and planning_____ 47
Interdependency_____ 50
Bars and charts_____ 52
Networks _____ 56
Resources _____ 61
Activity slack _____ 61
What did we do last time? _____ 62
Project planning with computers _____ 62
Summary _____ 64

5 Managing your project _____ 65
Management_____ 65
Managing projects vs day-to-day management _____ 66
Projects and managers _____ 67
Leaders and leadership_____ 68
Project managers and communication _____ 71
Project communications_____ 71
Project managers and negotiation _____ 72
Negotiating and bargaining _____ 73
Ways and means_____ 74
Project managers and motivation_____ 75
Summary _____ 77

6 Your project team_____ 78
Why teams? _____ 78
What is a team? _____ 79
Good teams and bad teams_____ 80

How many _____ 81
Who – and Why _____ 82
The Team Charter_____ 84
Team building_____ 85
Project teams _____ 87
Summary _____ 90

7 | **Managing your project money** _____ **92**
Money, money and money _____ 92
Cost, cost and more cost_____ 92
Hunches, guesstimates and estimates_____ 93
Information, data, facts and figures _____ 95
Top-down or bottom-up _____ 97
Top-down _____ 97
Bottom-up _____ 99
Below and above the line _____ 100
Budgets_____ 101
Summary _____ 103

8 | **Monitoring and controlling your project** ___ **104**
Full steam ahead_____ 104
Monitoring _____ 105
Project monitoring – what and when _____ 106
The project plan and monitoring _____ 108
Milestones _____ 109
Limits _____ 109
ABC analysis _____ 110
The project budget and monitoring _____ 111
Earned value_____ 112
Monitoring – reports and meetings _____ 114
Controlling _____ 115
Summary _____ 117

9 | **Solving your project problems**_____ **119**
Problems, problems and problems _____ 119
A perfect world_____ 120
Frequency and consequence_____ 120
Logic or intuition _____ 121
A Nominal Group_____ 122
Force Field analysis _____ 123

The Ishikawa diagram _____ 124
Pareto analysis _____ 126
CUSUM technique _____ 130
Summary _____ 132

10 Closing your project _____ 133
Endings _____ 133
Closure and the project manager _____ 134
The closure process _____ 135
Closing the team _____ 136
Closing the project data banks _____ 137
Activity completion _____ 138
Project outcomes _____ 139
Project histories _____ 140
Project audits _____ 141
Post-project appraisals _____ 142
Summary _____ 143

11 Key issues for project management _____ 144
Key issues _____ 144
Conclusion _____ 149

Glossary _____ 152

Further information _____ 157
Books _____ 157
Professional associations _____ 159
Some useful web sites _____ 161

Index _____ 162

ACKNOWLEDGEMENTS

Countless people have, often without realizing it, contributed to this book. For that reason I owe thanks to many – if not all – of the people that I've worked with in the past. They've all contributed, in one way or another. Special mention must be made though, of my agent, Teresa Chris; my publisher, Joanne Osborn at Hodder & Stoughton, London; Neil Kempshall of Robert Harding Computers in Brighton, England, and my partner, Linda Baguley – all of whose individual contributions have been particular.

Phil Baguley
Brighton, England
philb@pavilion.co.uk
Spring 1999

INTRODUCTION

This book is a readable and practical introduction to the craft of Project Management.

Written for all readers, it explains and illustrates the what, why, where, when and how of project management in an accessible and easily understood form. Jargon-free, based on sound theory, with diagrams, useful ideas and pointers to appropriate methods and tools it's *the* book for all of you who wish to begin to develop the skills of effective project management.

Managing a project is not an easy task. Nor, as we will see in the following chapters, is it one for the faint hearted. But managing a project well is not only satisfying and rewarding – it also enables you to develop and use skills that are transferable – skills that you can use to good effect elsewhere in your lives and careers.

Not all of your projects will be large and particular attention is paid in this book to the management of small projects. This sort of project abounds both in our workplaces – such as those involved in the process of performance improvement – and in our homes – as when we plan our holidays or remodel our houses. These are the small projects that you, as business professionals, managers or homeowners, are frequently involved in – often on a part-time basis.

By the time you get to the end of this book you will understand not only what a project is but also what you need to do to successfully plan, manage and control that project. By then, if not before, you should be ready to begin, with confidence, the process of managing your own projects. To reach that point you'll have threaded your way through the eleven chapters of this book. These chapters will tell you what is, and isn't, a project (Chapter 1); how to choose (Chapter 2), organize (Chapter 3), plan (Chapter 4), manage (Chapter 5) and monitor your project (Chapter 8) as well as how to assemble your project team (Chapter 6), manage your project money (Chapter 7), solve the problems that crop up along the way (Chapter 9) and, finally, how to close your project (Chapter 10).

Each of these chapters:

- starts with a brief summary of its objectives and content;
- contains accessible and understandable material that is easily related to your own experience and is full of useful ideas, pointers to appropriate methods, tools, diagrams and examples;
- finishes with a summary of its key points – all of which are reviewed in the book's final chapter (Chapter 11).

At the end of the book there's a glossary of useful project terms and a list of books and Internet web sites, all aimed at pointing you towards further, more advanced, material on project management.

But this isn't one of those books to be read and then put away – to gather dust on the shelf. It's a book aimed at enabling you to develop and enhance your ability to manage projects; a book to revisit – to dip into, refer to or browse over – as your project management experience and skill grow. Given half a chance, this book will give you one of the most powerful and flexible skills that you can possess – the ability to manage a project.

1 | **PROJECTS, PROJECTS AND PROJECTS**

This chapter begins our exploration of the what, why, where, when and how of projects. By the end of it, you'll have a clearer idea of what is a project, what its Five Fundamentals are, how the Three Dimensions define its boundaries, how the patterns of its life cycle vary and how the project differs from day-to-day management tasks.

Projects old and new

When the Egyptian Pharaoh Cheops died, in 2612 BC, he was buried in what we now call the Great Pyramid of Giza. Ranked as the tallest structure on Earth for over 43 centuries, this huge edifice took over twenty years and almost seven million person-weeks of effort to build. The finished structure contained over two million blocks of stone, each with an average weight of 2.5 tons. In its original form it rose some 146 metres above a square base whose sides are exactly aligned to the four points of the compass and measured almost 230 metres. A massive project – even by modern day standards – but not the only one in our history.

The 'top one hundred' list of humankind's projects includes other such ancient structures as the Colossus of Rhodes, the Coliseum of Rome, the Great Wall of China, the Mayan temples of Central America, the Pharos of Alexandria and the megalithic stone circle at Avebury, England. But the projects that led to these huge structures were rare, once in a generation, events.

Now, things are different. The project has become an every-day event. It's a regular feature of all our lives and for many of us it's a common-place experience to be involved in a project, either at work or at home. So why has this happened?

Projects now

Projects are about change. Without exception, they alter, modify, even transform the world in which we live. To do that they act in ways that are creative, energetic and active. The attraction of the project as a change-creating tool is both considerable and obvious. But this only goes part way to telling us why our use of the project has changed – why it has become a part of our every-day lives.

Part of the answer lies in the fact that we have all become more aware of the power of the project. For not only does the project create things, it also enables us to use our resources more efficiently and effectively. Today's business professional uses it to plan, direct and execute the ways in which organizational resources are used. In our homes we can use the project to enhance the quality of our lives. As a result the project has become a major contributor to survival and growth in all organizations, whatever their aims, products or services might be, and a tool for us all to use to shape our lives.

But this isn't the only reason. For the world has also changed. It is, for better or for worse, different from the one that our grandfathers and fathers lived and worked in. Our projects are bigger and more complex: NASA's Lunar Landing project, the Sydney Opera House, the 553 metre high CN tower in Toronto, the 3910 metre long Akashi–Kaikyo bridge in Japan, Hong Kong's new Chek Lap Kok international airport and China's huge Xiaolangdi dam on the Yellow River are all examples. They also have shorter life spans. In our market-places the tides of change are now global, rather than local or national. What happens in Tokyo on Monday is with us on Tuesday – if not before! This means that customer-led organizations, who need to respond to the desires of their customers, need a mechanism, a process, to enable them to do just that – and quickly.

The project is, without doubt, the answer to that need. It acts as a lens through which an organization or an individual can focus resources and abilities towards a desired outcome. In short, the project enables the organization to delight its customers and us, as individuals, to achieve our goals.

How and why

At the core of the project lies the act of doing. Projects are about work, actions, building, re-building, achievements, deliverables and outcomes.

But to be successful they must be managed with care and forethought – in ways that ensure that all of this 'doing' is carried out efficiently and effectively and focused towards a common endpoint. If we fail to do this then our projects will finish late, generate outcomes that are incomplete or inadequate and do so at costs that exceed our planned expenditure. These sorts of project – the failures of the project world – have ill-defined tasks and deliverables, and inappropriate organizations. They are poorly led, with ineffective communication systems and isolated project teams. Their plans are inflexible and inadequate. Successful projects plan and track measurable tasks and goals. They build on success in short-term deliverables to generate further successes in complex long-term outcomes. They look for results now, rather than later. Their problems are detected early; the creativity, commitment and energy of their teams drive their projects to success.

To make those things happen in our projects we need a map to help us steer our way, a framework from within which we can view the detail of the following chapters of this book, an image that tells us about the project process. The diagram in Figure 1.1 answers all these needs.

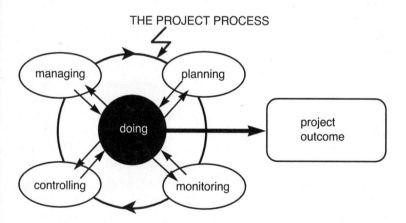

THE PROJECT PROCESS

Figure 1.1   The project process

Figure 1.1 not only confirms that the act of **doing** is core to the project process – it also tells us that it doesn't stand alone. For **doing** needs to be supported and reinforced by the acts of **managing**, **planning**, **monitoring** and **controlling**. But all of these need, if they are to be effective, to be carried out within an arena that is built on the foundations of good project management – which is where you come in.

But your involvement has its entry conditions.

For there are three criteria that you have to meet if you are going to become an effective, creative, change-generating project manager:

First: *You* have to *need* and *want* to be a project manager.
Second: *You* must have the opportunity – either at work or at home – to be able to explore being a project manager.
Third: *You* must have enough knowledge of the how and why of being a project manager.

The first two of these are down to you. The third one – the knowledge of the what, how, why and when of project management – is what this book is about. But first, before we reach out for that knowledge, what we need to do is to take a good hard look at the project itself.

Big or small

Most people will have heard about at least one big project. The ones that catch the public eye are usually about creating or doing things that are significant, large, expensive and well publicized, like NASA's Mars project or Football's World Cup.

But not all of our projects are as ambitious or as massive or as costly as these. For everyday, all over the world, millions of projects take place. They are launched, planned, monitored and completed with smaller outcomes, more modest costs and shorter time scales. New products are being launched, new books published, shops and restaurants 're-imaged' or 'restyled' and old or new businesses moved into new offices. The majority of these have deliverables that are modest, by any standards. For example, beverage vending machines are installed, customer record forms used by Sales Departments are modified, holidays are planned and taken.

If you cast your mind back you can probably remember a similar range of projects – from large to small or modest. It's also worth thinking about the numbers of people involved in those projects and you'll find that these too ranged from those involving many people – as when a company relocated – to those involving as few as two or three in a workplace or a family.

Concrete or ideas

If you ask most people about the projects that they remember, they'll probably tell you about the ones that had outcomes that were tangible. You could see, touch or get hold of them. But these concrete, tangible outcomes – like a new office block or a new computer – aren't the only sorts of outcome that our projects create.

For our projects can also be aimed towards far less tangible outcomes. These can be, for example, information about customers or changes in the ways in which we think or feel about a particular subject or issue. However, like their cousins with more concrete outcomes, they can still consume huge amounts of money and people time. Some of these are called 'influencing' projects. Examples include car manufacturers' advertising campaigns, aimed at persuading us to buy their newly launched cars; government or federal authority health campaigns, aimed at making us more aware of the risks of smoking or eating too much; and the campaigns of political parties, aimed at persuading us to vote for a particular candidate or party. In our workplaces this sort of 'influencing' project is often about such things as increasing quality, reducing waste or improving customer service. All of these are just as important as a new computer or a new office block. They all contain the potential to contribute to the effectiveness and efficiency of our organizations. In our homes these influencing projects can help us to support each other or try to persuade our children to behave better.

Work and play

The projects that you've heard of or worked on so far might lead you to believe that most of our projects are to do with our workplaces. But that isn't so. For the power of the project has spread out beyond the workplace into the rest of our lives. We all have individual projects. They can be about any part of our lives. Some of these are about our home – its size, features or decorations – while others are about our desire to be better swimmers, dancers, runners or golfers. Their outcomes can influence or change things like our own or our children's education, the sort of car we drive, how much we weigh or how we dress. You name it – it is, or has been, somebody's project.

These projects are just as important as our workplace projects. For not only are they statements of our individuality, their outcomes are also often very influential in our lives. They can, for example, result in us changing jobs, moving house, having an extension or sun-deck built, gaining a master's degree, having a holiday in Hawaii, changing or making-over the way we dress or do our hair, or even getting a new partner!

The Five Fundamentals

From what we've seen so far it's beginning to be pretty clear that the project is a versatile and powerful box of tricks.

It can:

- be about anything that we do or want to do
- be large or small – or any size in between
- last for decades – or be completed in a day
- cost any amount of money – from tens to billions
- create things that are either tangible or intangible.
- involve any number of people – from a single individual to nations.

And yet, despite this astonishing range of outcomes, sizes, costs and durations, *all* of these projects have a number of basic characteristics in common.

These, the **Five Fundamentals**, are present in all our projects:

1 Projects are one-time efforts

All projects are one-off events. They come and go, appear and disappear, leaving behind the often, all too concrete product of their labours. In this, they are very different from the repetitive activities of our day-to-day work. The project's activities begin, the project workload grows from modest beginnings to reach a peak of activity and then the project fades away leaving outcomes that are, as we will soon see, unique.

2 Projects are unique

No two projects are exactly alike. Every project, whatever its outcome, has at its core something that is singular to that particular project. In some projects this singularity or uniqueness is considerable. They have never-to-be-repeated outcomes – like the Pyramids in Egypt or the Thames

Flood Barrier in London. In other projects, however, this uniqueness is less obvious and even seems to be masked by the similarities between it and other projects. For example, a project to build yet another office block in Sydney appears, on the surface, to be the same as all the other office block projects in that city. But it *is* unique – it has a different design, different contractors, different site, different client, different foundations, different access, etc., etc.

3 Projects have limited and defined time spans

A project is about the creation of something by a specific time. It has a 'deadline' or target completion date. This means that the project doesn't go on for ever. It reaches a point in time when it is complete. When this happens the project is closed, its management team is disbanded and its people move on to other projects or other tasks. The project outcome is handed over to those who are to manage its day-to-day operations. On larger and more complex projects, this time span might cover several years – even decades. It took fourteen years to create the Statue of Liberty! But even these projects reach an end-point.

4 Projects are about change

All projects are about change. They create the new and sometimes knock down the old. These changes can be large or small and can have either trivial or significant implications for our lives. They change the places in which we work and the ways in which we do that work. Managing this change requires special skills. These are skills that are quite different from those needed to maintain the relative stability and predictability of day-to-day operations.

5 Projects have defined outcomes

All projects have well-defined deliverables. These might be a newly built house, a just-published book, a changed business structure, a newly purchased car or victory in a campaign to be elected to a political office. The pathways to these outcomes consist of linked chains of activities. Each of these might have a sub-goal or sub-outcome, as, for example, when building a house we have to have a sub-goal of completing the foundations. This, as we will see in later chapters, helps the ways in which we plan, control and manage the project. As the project progresses, these sub-goals often become increasingly interdependent. That is, they require other tasks to be completed before they, in their turn, can be completed. For example, in our house project, we have to complete both the foundations and the walls of the house before we can put its roof on. In the end, all of these sub-goals or sub-outcomes must be completed in order to achieve the project's overall goal or outcome.

These Five Fundamentals are present in all projects, whatever their size, cost or duration.

Definitions

This is the point in the book at which we need to decide exactly what we mean by a 'project'. In other words, we need to produce a definition of a project.

When it comes to definitions, dictionaries are always a good place to start. The *Oxford English Dictionary* tells us that a project is 'something projected or proposed for execution; a plan, scheme, purpose; a proposal' – which, as far as it goes, is concise and to the point. But does it go far enough? Does it, for example, tell us about the project's uniqueness, its limited duration or its specified outcome? The answer, of course, is no, it doesn't.

But when we look at the literature of project management we find little improvement. Some writers stress the uncertainty of projects and write about 'risk' and 'steps in to the unknown', while others speak eloquently of 'human endeavour', specific outcomes or simply beginnings and ends. None of these really capture the essence of a project that, as we saw earlier, embodies uniqueness and definitive statements about duration and outcomes.

So, to get out of this log-jam, we'll have to generate our own definition. From this point onwards, this is what we'll mean when we use the word 'project':

A project is a sequence of connected events that are conducted over a defined and limited period of time and are targeted towards generating a unique but well defined outcome.

When we apply this to our earlier examples of projects, we find that they all fit – they all display a degree of uniqueness, consist of activities that are connected to each other and have defined outcomes and limited time spans. This means that we can now begin to view the project as a tool – one that we can use to achieve outcomes and create deliverables. We can, for example, use the project at work to introduce a new management information system, change the way we record the details of our customers, restructure our organization, target a new market niche or influence the ways in which our people think about quality. In our homes we can use the project to restyle our bedrooms, create our sun-decks and plan where we go for our holidays.

But let's not run away with the idea that the project is the only tool that's available to us. Most of us have a whole range of change-creating tools in our kit-bag. However, none of these is as powerful or as effective as the project. But, as is so with all tools, the skill comes in knowing *when* to use the project but, perhaps more importantly, *how* to use it. The next step towards that knowledge comes when we begin to explore the contours of our projects – when we find out more about their boundaries.

The project boundaries

One of the most obvious things about a project is its outcome. Indeed, this is so obvious, that many of us fall into the trap of thinking that it is the only feature of a project. We identify projects by their outcomes, as in NASA's Mars Landing project or Hong Kong's new Chek Lap Kok international airport project, and forget that all projects have other key and inter-related features.

When we ask questions these features begin to emerge. 'How long did it take?' or 'How much did it cost?' and 'Was the final outcome as we specified it at the beginning' and, finally, and most importantly 'Does that outcome do what we wanted it to?' are all questions about the other key features of the project. All of these are equally important; their dimensions define the boundaries of our projects. They also exert a considerable influence upon ways in which we manage them. For example, the question 'How long did it take?' raises the issue of the time span of the overall project or the individual activities that make it up. 'How much did it cost?' draws our attention to the cost of the project. 'Was the outcome as specified at the beginning?' and 'Did the outcome do what we wanted it to?' are both about the project's performance as seen in its outcome.

But none of these features stands alone. They are all woven together in a complex web of inter-relatedness. As such it is possible to have trade-offs between them; as, for example, when getting it done more quickly costs more or when adding more features costs more and takes longer.

Additionally, the Quality Revolution, with its emphasis on customer satisfaction, means that we now have to be aware of the need to extend our definition of the project's performance to include the quality or 'Fitness for Purpose' of its outcome.

These three features or dimensions – **Time**, **Cost** and **Performance** – are key to all of our projects.

We need to be aware of them when we define, manage, plan, monitor and control our project. For example, a project to build a sports stadium would be defined in terms of its **Performance** – as in the size of its running track and playing field, the changing facilities, size of car park, etc.; its **Cost** – $30,000,000 and **Time**, i.e. its duration – to be ready for use by 1 December 2010. The quality aspects of this Performance relate this project to the needs of the customer and can be expressed in terms of both individual and idiosyncratic factors. These will be objective, such as 'Are there enough parking spaces?' and subjective, such as ' Is the warm-up area big enough?' Think back to when you last bought something major – a house, a car or even an office block – and see if you can recognize the importance of this subjectivity and the ways in which it influences your decisions.

These three dimensions – **Time**, **Cost** and **Performance** – mark the boundaries of our project (see Figure 1.2). As such they must be clearly and unambiguously defined at the beginning of the project. We must know, for example, how much money we have, when the project must be complete and what the characteristics of its outcome are. These must also be monitored throughout the project's lifetime. If we fail to do this, then we will be unable to either manage or control them and this, without doubt, will lead to failure.

Figure 1.2   The three dimensions – Time, Cost and Performance

The project life cycle

The idea of the life cycle is a familiar one. We all experience birth, growth, adulthood, old age and death at one time or another. In fact, it's such a basic idea that it's often applied in all sorts of areas. In marketing, for example, it's used to explain the ways in which the sales of a product rise and fall over its lifetime in the market place. In quality assurance, it's used to describe how the reliability of a piece of equipment varies with its age.

So, can we apply it to the project?

Well, like us, projects also have beginnings and ends. They also have periods of growth – phases in which their consumption of money and other resources rises. These are followed by periods of stability and then decline, in which their consumption of resources also changes. Activity rates expand from small beginnings to reach maturity and then diminish and ultimately fall away. In the simplest version of the project life cycle, these are called the Beginning, the Intermediate and the Final phases. But these names don't tell us very much. They don't, for example, tell us what goes on in those phases or what their outcomes are. When we look at the human life cycle we see that its phases have names which tell us what's happening then, such as childhood, adolescence, adulthood, middle age, old age.

The names that we will use in the project life cycle will do the same:

Feasibility phase – in which the idea of the project is conceived, its broad objectives identified, its feasibility reviewed and its initial estimates of cost, performance and time are generated. By the end of this phase our embryonic project has been compared with other projects or assessed against standards of performance. A go/no go decision will have been made – to implement, or not. A 'go' decision leads on to the next stage of the project life cycle, Planning and Design, while a 'no go' decision will lead to the project being put aside, to appear again, perhaps, at the next spending round. A minority of projects pass this stage and Chapter 2 describes how that choice is made.

Planning and Design phase – in which growth – developing the detail of the project and its outcome, deciding who will do what and when – takes place. The cost and time estimates of the project are refined. Decisions are made about who should be awarded the major contracts of the project by the end of this phase. Activity rates in this period are, however, still relatively low.

Production phase – in which most things happen, activity rates reach their peak and most of the planned work takes place. Effective monitoring and control procedures are needed in this phase. They tell the project manager what has or hasn't been done or spent, what ought to have been done or spent and what will need to be done or spent in the time that's left. By the end of this stage the project's outcome is substantially complete and ready to be handed over to those who will use it.

Termination phase – in which the project is audited and reviewed and the project team is broken up.

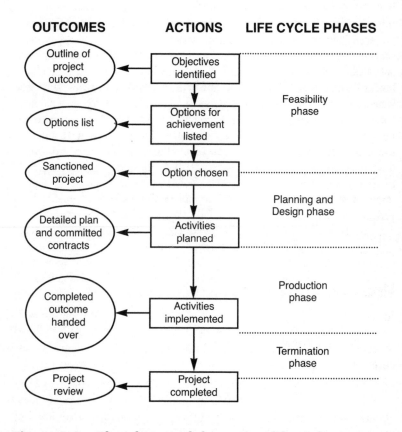

Figure 1.3   The phases of the project life cycle

We can see that the rates at which things are done change throughout this cycle. This leads to differing and varying resource demands. For most projects, the Production phase, with its focus on getting things done, involves the peak level of resource demands.

Project priorities

As a project moves through this life cycle, what is important changes. These changes influence the position of the project relative to its boundaries; boundaries whose dimensions are, as we saw earlier, measured in terms of **Time**, **Cost** and **Performance**.

Initially, in the Feasibility phase, these are all of equal ranking and the project is, as it were, equidistant from all three boundaries. As the project survives the rigours of the selection process and moves into the Planning and Design phase, Time becomes more important, taking the lead from Performance and Cost in joint second place. This is not surprising when we realize that most of the initial scheduling and planning decisions are taken during this stage. When we enter the next phase – Production, with its focus on 'getting things done' – the focus of the project shifts initially towards Performance and then, towards the end of this phase, back towards Time. But by the end of this phase the project will have returned to a position that rates Time, Cost and Performance to be of equal importance. This continues through the Termination phase.

Despite these changes in relative importance, all of these aspects are important and none of them should be neglected if you want to achieve the final outcome of a successful project.

Projects and people

In the end, projects are about people. Their creativity, adaptability and energy are needed to plot, plan and manage the project's course. They are involved and interested – as project team members, as clients or as customers, even as the proverbial man or woman on the street – in the project's processes or outcomes. All of these people are, in one way or another, entangled with the project. As such they are project stakeholders.

To be a project stakeholder you have to have something to gain or lose by the way the project turns out or have an interest, however indirect, in the success or failure of the project. This throws the net in a wide arc. For example, a government-funded project with the outcome of a new hospital will have a list of stakeholders that includes medical and non-medical employees, community doctors, volunteers, suppliers, patients, project team members, local elected representatives, the community, project manager, social services staff, regional health authority, government agencies, contractors and sub-contractors and taxpayers.

It won't take long for you to see that some of these stakeholders have interests that are in opposition. A patient, for example, wants the best possible hospital, irrespective of cost, while the government agency is concerned with issues such as value for money and spend limitation. Nevertheless, all stakeholders are important and finding ways of resolving the conflicts between their often, very different needs and demands is one of the major challenges that faces the project manager.

Summary

The project is a way of creating change. Its outcomes can be tangible or intangible. Projects can be large or small, involve any number of people and have life spans of days, years or decades. All projects have at their core the act of **doing** – which is supported and reinforced by the acts of **managing**, **planning**, **monitoring** and **controlling**. The Five Fundamentals define our projects – they are all one-off events that involve a sequence of connected activities that take place over a limited period of time and are targeted to generate a unique but well-defined outcome. The dimensions of the project's boundaries are expressed in terms of **Time**, **Cost** and **Performance** – all of which must be clearly and unambiguously defined at the beginning of the project and managed and controlled throughout its duration. Projects have life cycles with the four phases of Feasibility, Planning and Design, Production and Termination. Each of these has activity rates, resource demands and outcomes that are different. Finally, all projects are about people – stakeholders – who need to be involved in the project's change process if it is to be successful.

2 | WHICH PROJECT?

There are always more suitors than bridegrooms in the project sanction stakes. Most of us have to justify our proposed projects to others and this chapter looks at the ways in which the 'chosen few' are selected. By the end of this chapter you will have a better understanding of the way that choice is made and the factors, such as risk and uncertainty, that influence it.

Choice

A project, as we saw in the last chapter, is an active agent for change. But the change that the project brings is not an accidental, 'fall of the dice', event. On the contrary, it is the result of a deliberate, pre-determined, sequence of actions. These are a part of a project that has been intentionally chosen, often from a number of alternatives.

This step of choosing which project to implement, or not to implement, is a significant one. For not only can the choice made give life to our embryonic project, the way that it is made can also influence its chances of successful completion. For if our projects are to be successful, then they have to be chosen well. A poorly chosen project is always a candidate for failure, irrespective of how we manage, plan and control it. Reviews of failed projects tell us that, for most of them, the seeds of their failure were sown in the selection process. If we are to avoid failure for our projects, then we need to choose them with care – with a clear understanding of the risks and uncertainties involved.

However, for most of us, our role in this project selection process is that of suitor rather than judge. In our workplaces we have to present our potential projects to committees of decision-takers or to the company owner or general manager. In our homes we are faced with the demands of others for the time and money needed by our projects. We have to justify the structure and content of our projects; we have to argue for their right to live and grow. To do this effectively we need to understand this process of project selection, a process that is influenced by two factors.

The first of these reflects the environment in which we live and work. In this, there are, and always will be, alternatives to all of our actions. These sprout like many-headed hydra along the pathways of our lives. The choice of what alternative to follow is one that is often determined by resource demands. Since these resources are often limited, the answers to questions such as 'What will it cost?' or 'How many people does it need?' or 'How much will we save?' are often key to the decisions made about our potential projects.

The second of these factors is about information. We never, ever, have enough of the 'right' information when we need it. Despite our computer systems and databases, it's always yesterday's data. And this brings us face to face with the uncertainties and risks of our projects.

Uncertainty and risk

Uncertainty, and its cousin, risk, will always be with us. There will always be alternatives that we hadn't thought about, events that we hadn't foreseen and information that wasn't available when we needed it. All of these uncertainties create risk. For example, when we launch a new product we face uncertainty about whether it will sell. We take the risk that the investments that we make to create that product will not pay off. Similarly, when we reorganize our homes we face uncertainty as to whether the revised layout will be as comfortable and as functionally effective as the old one. This means that we put at risk the investment that we make in time, labour and money to achieve that reorganization.

For many people, uncertainty and risk are negative and anxiety-provoking. Their instincts tell them to delay, to step aside from situations where these abound, to strike out for the high ground of apparent certainty. But, as is so with many things in the field of human endeavour, these things are relative. For what is risk to us can represent opportunity to others and what is threatening and uncertain to some can be challenging to us. When we face up to uncertainty and risk, while others turn away, then we open up an opportunity to gain advantage. Our new product may then be a runaway success or our home layout may be all that we desired it to be.

But these ventures can never be free from risk. What we can do, however, is to reduce or limit the influence that risk exerts on our project. By doing this we not only increase the project's chances of success, we also increase our ability to manage it effectively.

To do this we need to:

- **Identify** the type, level and source of foreseeable risk
- **Reduce or eliminate** that risk
- **Decide** whether or not we will accept the remaining risk.

This three-stage sequence lies at the core of the larger process of project selection.

Identify the risk

Finding out what are the nature, level and source of our project's risks can take time. But it is worth doing.

We can do it by looking at the two Cs – Cause and Consequence. We can look at the causes of these risks and then at their consequences – as in what might happen and what would then follow if it did happen – or we can look at their consequences and then at their causes – as in what is an undesirable outcome and how might it be caused.

An example of the first of these, looking first at a cause and then at its consequences, occurs when we ask 'What happens if the bricks (to build our house) aren't delivered on time?' The consequences that would follow are then identified and listed. These could include delay or non-completion for both the overall project and for the individual tasks that are dependent upon a timely delivery of bricks or the timely completion of another task that needed those bricks.

When we look at the second of these types of risk analysis, the one that looks at consequences first and then identifies the possible causes, we might start by asking 'What might cause us to be unable to tile the roof of our house?' We would then go on to list the possible causes: both direct, as when the tiles aren't delivered on time; and indirect, as when the roof timber installation was delayed by bad weather.

Another way of identifying the nature and level of the project's risk is to use a risk matrix as in Figure 2.1.

What this matrix tells us is that if our project has an outcome that has been successfully achieved in the past, 'Been done before', and that the ways that we intend to use to achieve it are well proven, also 'Been done before', then we have a low risk project. However, if we intend to build our house using new and unproven methods of construction, 'Never been done before', or build a house with a very novel design or use new 'high-tech' materials, also 'Never been done before', then the risk level of the project will rise.

Project change process

	Been done before	Never been done before
Been done before **Project outcome** **Never been done before**	LOW RISK MODERATE RISK	MODERATE RISK HIGH RISK

Figure 2.1 Identifying a project's risk using a risk matrix

But it's not enough just to identify the nature, level and source of our project's risks, we need to do something about them.

Reducing the risk

Once we know what are the level and nature of our project's risks, then we need to make a judgement as to whether or not they will happen.

Again we need to look at the two Cs – Cause and Consequence. We can either estimate the likelihood of the cause happening or estimate the likelihood of the consequence occurring once the cause has happened. The easiest ways of doing this involve either comparing them to other similar risks or drawing from our experience of identical or similar risks. For our house-building project, this would tell us that brick deliveries are routine events and, providing sufficient notice is given, the delivery of standard bricks is an event with a low likelihood of failure.

The level and amount of information that we need to make these estimates changes with our position in the project choice process. In the earliest part of the Feasibility phase of the project's life cycle, the objectives of the project will be expressed in broad and general terms and a low level of detail will suffice. Later, when comparisons are being made with other projects, a higher level of detail will be needed.

This also changes when we look at both the nature and probability of the risk's potential consequences. For example, the reactor of a town centre nuclear power plant may be likely to explode once in five hundred years. That is, it is a low probability event. But if it does explode it would cause the deaths of several million people. This combination of the probability of a risk occurring and the consequences of its occurrence helps us. It gives us, even if we have to guess the probability, a basis on which we can decide whether or not to attempt to reduce the risk. For example, if either the probability of the risk occurring is high or the consequences of the risk are unacceptable then we have to attempt to reduce them. To do this we will need further data. But it's not just any old data. For the scope and outcomes of this data-gathering need to reflect both the anticipated value of outcomes and the likely quality and accuracy of the information gained.

Once we have generated these estimates then we can use them to help us evaluate our risks.

At this stage – when the choice is about which project to proceed with – this sort of risk evaluation is generally concerned with the more general, broad brush, issues, rather than the fine detail. Questions such as 'Have we done this before?', 'Has this happened before?' or 'Have we done this in this place before?' might be asked to assess the level of risk involved. One of the ways by which these questions can be answered is by small multi-disciplinary study teams whose objectives are to weed out bad or faulty ideas, identify 'dead ends', and produce a clear assessment of risk and benefit together with recommendations about what to do next. Prototypes and trials can also figure in this information gathering process; a prototype being a first attempt to create a key part of the project outcome, while a trial involves exposing the prototype to users. Both of these cost money and take up time, but they can be cheaper in the long run than the failure that might occur if they were not used. For using them provides us with not only more information about the risks of our project but also the information that we need to reduce those risks.

Yes or No

We have identified the source, nature and level of our project risk and done all that we can to reduce it. Now we have to make a decision – about whether or not to proceed with that particular project.

But risk isn't the only factor that influences this decision.

For example, an organization that is unusually profitable may be prepared to spend A$400,000 on a speculative high risk project while an organization with much lower profits would not. Similarly, a non profit-making organization will fund projects which contribute to the effectiveness of its use of scarce or expensive resources – such as capital or people – while a profit-making organization will be concerned with only profitability or the change in its competitive position that results from a project.

The amount of capital available for projects can also vary. It can be a fixed amount, with a consequence of intense competition between projects and the implementation of what is termed 'capital rationing', or it can be unlimited, so that all projects whose marginal cost equals their marginal return are funded. In reality, however, we usually need more money than we have. This means that our estimate of the capital needs of our project can be crucially influential in whether or not it is chosen. The accuracy of this estimate varies, as we will see in Chapter 7, according to our position in the project life cycle.

The factors that affect our choice of which project to implement are diverse and various. They include influences such as legislation, interest rates, the actions of competitors and the industrial relations climate of our organizations. Not the least of these influences are the interests and needs of the project stakeholders who, as we saw in Chapter 1, all have something to gain or lose by the way that the decision about their particular project turns out.

Choosing

The decision as to which project to implement is a conscious and formal one. In large organizations it is often taken by a group of senior managers. This decision-taking group is often called a 'capital investment committee', because of its role in controlling and allocating the often limited amount of capital available for projects. In some organizations, however, its title can reflect the outcome of the projects – as in the 'publishing committee' of a book publisher or the 'new products' group of a detergent manufacturer. In smaller organizations the decision to implement or not to implement a project is often taken by individuals such as the company owner or the organization's general manager. The range and number of alternative projects considered in these smaller companies may be small. In our homes the decision-taking process is less formal, involving some or all of the family group.

The techniques that are used to help make this decision are both numerical and non-numerical in nature. We can, for example, make our choice on the basis of the time needed to pay back the initial capital investment or by using sophisticated accounting concepts such as Net Present Value (see page 27). We may also use non-numerical techniques that allow us to express our intuition or preferences. These techniques are versatile enough to be used in a wide variety of situations. We can use them, for example, to decide which make and type of washing machine we wish to purchase for our home, which size, type and make of delivery van to purchase for our small business, which research project to invest in or which site on which to locate our new factory.

Under all of these circumstances each of the alternatives will have different costs, benefits and risks. These are rarely known with absolute certainty. This uncertainty and other factors are brought to bear upon our choice of which project to implement and that choice is, as we saw earlier, a key step in the process of managing a successful project.

Choosing without numbers

There will always be situations in which projects arise without enough supporting information. This might happen, for example, when we need to react quickly to circumstances or when the information is just not available or when we don't have time to generate it. When this happens we still need to evaluate the project but, from necessity, can only do so on a subjective rather than an objective basis.

Some examples of when and how this is done are as follows.

Floods, storms, hurricanes and other crises

When our factory, shop, office or home is threatened by an oncoming storm, flood or hurricane or when the freezer breaks down, we need to do something about it. We may, for example, need to buy storm shutters or boards to protect our shop windows, build a protective dyke to divert flood water away from our home or buy a new freezer. In these circumstances a formal project evaluation is not only impractical – it's also irrelevant.

What can help are the answers to simple questions such as 'Is the factory worth protecting, and if so, at what cost?' If the damage does occur then the question changes to 'Is the factory or office worth repairing, and if so, at what cost?' If the answer is no, then we need to create a new project for a replacement facility. If the answer is yes, that is, that we do need to repair the damage in order to stay in business, then the focus of the project's control will be on the required current expenditure rather than on meeting the budget. However, even this expenditure will have its limits, the most obvious being that you wouldn't spend more in repair costs than the value of the shop or factory.

Legal necessity

Our governments, state legislatures and federal agencies all generate laws, codes, statutory rules and regulations that tell us what we can and cannot do in our organizations and homes. These are often subject to change or reinterpretation.

As a consequence the ways in which we operate businesses and what we do in our places of work or homes may also have to change. These are mandatory projects – we have little choice about whether we do, or don't, implement them. Again the focus of the management of this type of project is not on estimation of the costs but on the control of the required expenditure. Examples of this sort of project might include the provision of ventilation equipment to limit employee's exposure to fumes, the provision of wrist supports or special keyboards to prevent RSI (Repetitive Strain Injury), the removal of asbestos from our houses or the provision of access for the disabled.

Canteens and car parks

Some of our projects are about such things as staff canteens, sports facilities or car parking facilities. In our organizations these are called employee welfare projects and they are generally created, sanctioned and implemented as a result of an organization's human resources policy. They rarely, if ever, generate a financial return of any sort and can involve high levels of capital spend. They do, nevertheless, require careful management, monitoring and control.

Sacred cow projects

These projects come about because of the power and influence of senior managers or senior members of the family. In our organizations they can have beginnings that are as modest as the CEO (Chief Executive Officer) asking 'Why don't we have a look a ...', or beginnings which are as complex as an individual manager's need to prove his or her suitability for a more senior role by his or her patronage of projects with a rapid effect on annual profit. Their selection can often be surrounded with 'political' intrigue ànd might even bypass the formal project selection procedures. The best of them, however, may reflect the intuition or 'gut feel' of experienced, capable and powerful managers. In our families, their roots are, if anything, even more complex.

Competitive advantage

In today's fiercely competitive and often volatile business environment, competitive advantage can make a significant contribution to an organization's profitability. When a project is seen to have this potential it needs to be sanctioned quickly so that it enters the marketplace ahead of any rival and, if successful, maximizes the profit generated. These 'fast-track' projects are not without their risks – risks that could be reduced by feasibility studies or prototyping. Nevertheless, once sanctioned, they do need careful management and control.

Ranking

Comparative ranking is a technique that is often used to help us choose between a number of similar projects. Often used when we have limited or no quantitative information about these projects, it relies on our ranking them, relative to each other, under a number of headings. The project with the best total ranking is then chosen for implementation. The headings chosen must be equally applicable to all the projects but will, of course, reflect the nature of these projects. For example, a comparison between different sites for a new factory will have headings that include road and rail access, labour availability, ease of construction and availability of utilities; while a comparison between the different sorts of passenger car might use factors such as capital cost, maintenance cost, insurance cost, ease of parking, load-bearing capacity, ease of passenger entry and exit and fuel costs. The ranking matrix generated to compare three alternatives would rank each of them against the others and award each a rating – in this case 1 being the best and 3 being the worst. The overall best of these alternatives will then have the lowest total score.

The advantages of this sort of process include its speed and ease of application and its need for 'better or worse than' assessments rather than absolute numbers.

'Nice to do' projects

These are the 'spur of the moment' holidays, the unplanned weekends in New York, Sydney or Las Vegas or the impromptu shopping trips on London's Oxford Street. These are often unplanned and spontaneous and as such not subject to any comparison with alternatives. We undertake these projects because they are simply 'nice to do'. They rarely generate any financial return and can involve high levels of spend. They do, nevertheless, require careful management to maximize the pleasure and enjoyment that we gain from them.

Choosing by numbers

Money is a scarce commodity and this, together with the complexity and size of the costs, consequences, risks and potential profits of many of our projects, means that we often evaluate these projects by using numbers.

Examples of how this can be done are as follows.

Payback period method

The payback period for a project is the period of time that it takes for the project outcome to repay its initial capital investment. For example, a project which cost 100,000 Rand to implement may have an annual profit of 25,000 Rand. The payback period for this project is:

$$\text{Payback period} = \frac{100,000}{25,000} = 4 \text{ years}$$

The project with the shortest payback period is the one that is chosen. Payback period is a simple and easy-to-use method which is appropriate for low-cost projects. When we apply it to high-cost or long-time-span projects we do come up against some of its limitations – like the fact that it assumes that cash flows after the payback period are of no interest or that money doesn't change in value as time passes.

Rate of return method

This method looks at the rate of return that the project outcome generates from the capital invested in it. The project with the highest rate of return is the one that is chosen. The rate of return, which is usually expressed as a percentage figure, is found by dividing the annual profit by the implementation cost.

In our earlier example the rate of return is:

$$\frac{\text{Annual profit}}{\text{Implementation cost}} \times 100 = \frac{25,000}{100,000} \times 100 = 25\%$$

This is a simple and easy-to-use method. It is best applied to low-cost, short-time-scale projects, and generates an average rate of return for the period considered. It also suffers from its assumption that the value of money doesn't change with time.

Net Present Value (NPV) or Discounted Cash Flow (DCF) method

Discounting is a way of determining today's value for money that will be earned in the future. It is the opposite of compounding which tells us the future value of today's cash flows. When we use discounting in our project selection process it enables us to ignore factors like the changing values of the project's goods and equipment. DCF or NPV allows for the fact that the value of money does change with time by converting all of the future earnings of a project to their present-day value.

It does this by using this equation:

$$\text{Net Present Value} = \left[\text{Total of} \frac{\text{Future value cash flow}}{(1 + \text{interest rate})^n} \right] - \text{Capital invested}$$

where: – n is the number of years
    – values of $1/(1 + \text{interest rate})^n$ can be found in books of discounting tables.

This means that for a project with an assumed interest rate of 10%, an implementation cost of $4,000 and projected profit pattern of:

Year number	1	2	3	4
Annual Profit ($)	1,200	1,500	1,400	1,600

we can calculate its net present value like this:

Year number	1	2	3	4
Value of $1/(1+r)^n$	.9091	.8264	.7513	.6830
Annual Profit ($)	1,200	1,500	1,400	1,600
Present Value of Annual Profit ($)	1,091	1,240	1,052	1,093

This gives us a total present value of Annual Profits of $4,476. This exceeds the implementation cost of $4,000 by $476. When this happens the project is acceptable because the value of the organization will increase. The greater the increase, the more worthwhile is the project. If the reverse is true and the value of the sum of these discounted future cash flows or present values of future annual profits is less than the implementation cost then the project should be rejected, as the value of the organization will fall.

Profitability Index

The Profitability Index – sometimes called the Benefit-Cost Ratio – is the ratio of the sum of the net present values to the capital required for implementation. If the value of this ratio exceeds 1.0 then the project is acceptable. The higher the value is, the more acceptable the project is. In the example given above the Profitability Index would have been $4,476/ $4,000 or 1.119.

Internal Rate of Return

This method of assessing projects discounts the future annual profits of the project over a range of interest rates and then calculates the NPV (for a given period of time) for each of those rates. As the interest rate rises, the NPV falls. The interest rate at which the NPV becomes zero is called the Internal Rate of Return (see Figure 2.2). The higher the interest rate is, the better the project. The choice of whether to implement a project is based on whether this Internal Rate of Return exceeds the cost to the organization of borrowing capital. If it does then the project is acceptable. If it is below this borrowing cost, then the project will be rejected.

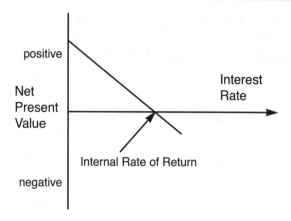

Figure 2.2   Internal rate of return

Summary

At the beginning of this chapter we saw that all projects involve risk and uncertainty. The two Cs – Cause and Consequence – are involved in the three steps at the heart of the project selection process. These steps involve, first, identifying the type, level and source of that risk, then, reducing it, and finally, deciding whether or not to accept it. Projects can be chosen by non-numerical methods as in their ability to answer the demands of crises, legal requirements, employee welfare needs, individual's power or status needs, the organization's competitive needs and, last but not least, because they are 'nice to do'. Relative ranking is a non-numerical method while payback period, rate of return, net present value, profitability index and internal rate of return are numerical methods.

3 | YOUR PROJECT ORGANIZATION

Projects need to be organized. By the end of this chapter you should have a better understanding of how you can do this. You should also be able to see why you need project documentation such as the project specification, role and responsibility definitions, budgets, accounts and change control procedures.

Organizing

Organizing is something that we all do, or try to do, quite often. We organize our holidays, we organize our homes, we organize our days out and we organize our offices. The act of organizing seems woven into the warp and weft of our lives.

So what is it and what do we hope to achieve by doing it?

Put simply, when we organize things we systematize them. We bring things, that were separate, together in ways that are orderly and systematic. When we do this we create a new whole with structure. For example, when we organize a children's birthday party, the things that we bring together are food, drinks, presents and guests. The whole that we create – the party – has a structure, with times and places for playing games, blowing out the candles on the birthday cake, eating jelly, opening presents, etc. The food, drinks, presents and guests all act together to create the outcome we desire – a happy and memorable social occasion that celebrates a child's birthday.

When we organize a project the things that we bring together are:

- **information** – about the project's outcome, nature, duration, cost and quality; about the client
- **people** – with their skills, creativity, needs, experience and abilities
- **resources** – such as materials, equipment, money and time.

The whole, within which these can act together to create the desired outcome, is our project organization.

But not all the things that we organize are as short-lived or as modest as a birthday party. Some last for decades and involve throngs of people. They provide the connections and co-ordination that are necessary for many of the functions of our society. Their value is such that they achieve virtual permanence as the cornerstones of our societies. These, our organizations are the dominant forms of our society.

Organizations

Organizations exist everywhere and embrace every aspect of our lives. They educate our children, collect our rubbish, sell us goods or services, govern our communities and countries, fight our wars for us and provide us with jobs. Most of us spend the greater part of our lives working in organizations of one sort or another. All the groups, clubs, establishments or societies in which we work and play are organizations. Indeed, some sociologists tell us that the family is a form of organization.

These organizations vary enormously in both size and complexity. They can be small, consisting of limited numbers of people with a common interest, such as playing golf or chess, or they can be huge, complex and powerful, as with our governments or the conglomerates that provide so many of the goods and services that we consume. All of these have ambitions, goals or objectives and they all husband and use scarce resources towards the end of achieving them.

Given all of this, it is not surprising to find that the relationship between the project and the organization is an important one. Organizations, in one form or another, supply the equipment and materials that the project uses, they fund its activities, they train and educate its people and they represent the interests of the diverse and separate groups of stakeholders who wish to influence the project's outcome. But, most importantly, they are the clients for whom many of our projects are created and managed. Because of this we need, albeit briefly, to take a look at the structure and characteristics of the organization itself.

Structures, leaders and people

The structures of our organizations show considerable variety. They range from being highly ordered, with several levels of power and formally defined roles, to being very fluid, almost organic in form, with very limited formality or hierarchy.

Despite this diversity, all these organizations are made up of individuals. These individuals have chosen to come together because they have a common need, desire, purpose or interest. The resulting organizations are usually arranged in ways that are systematic. These systems – which can be both formal and informal – are mainly concerned with the ways in which the organization's resources, such as materials, money, information, etc., are used and the ways in which power and influence are exerted. As a result, our organizations have:

■ **leaders** – to act as a focus for our diverse individual interests and efforts
■ **structures** – with roles and responsibilities
■ **procedures** – which are aimed at ensuring that resources are effectively deployed towards the achievement of the organization's objectives.

But what about the people of these organizations? Organizations need people. Indeed, organizations *are* people. People bring organizations to life; they make them work, despite their often considerable complexity. Even if we have the best of leaders, the most refined structures and the best procedures, we still need that other vital ingredient – people. Without people, a leader cannot lead and without people's support and compliance, the structures and procedures of the organization might as well be written in sand.

The survival of an organization depends upon its ability to adapt and change in the face of the winds of change. Projects, as we saw in Chapter 1, can answer that need. But if these are to be successful, if they are to help our organizations to adapt, then they too must be organized and this must be done in ways that are compatible with the structures and systems of those organizations. This isn't always easy to achieve – as we will now see.

Projects and organizations – the differences

When we first compare projects and organizations we find that they appear to have much in common. They both, for example, have desired outcomes or objectives and they both have leaders, structures, systems and procedures. However, there are differences – differences that are key to the ways in which the project is organized and managed, and key to the ways in which we make sure that the project and the organization are compatible.

The first of these is about time horizons. We already know from the Five Fundamentals that the project has a defined and limited life span. Its time horizon doesn't extend beyond the point at which its outcome is handed over to its client. The organization, however, has no such limits. Its ambitions are long term; they extend over the horizon of the future and are, above all, about survival and continued existence. In contrast, the project, despite the often solid and considerable nature of its outcomes, is ephemeral. It is here for a short while and then gone – like the dragon-fly of summer. Its objectives are time specific: they must be achieved by a certain date or time, one that is known at its birth. Once this is achieved then the project will voluntarily terminate.

But that's not the only difference. We also know that the outcome of each project is unique, singular and one-off. But this isn't true of the organization. Its outcomes are replicas of an original that was created at some point in its history. These replicas can be, like the project's outcomes, tangible or intangible, but they are still replicas. The organization's prime concern is to ensure that it can continue to – repeatedly and accurately – produce, generate or provide these replicas. These may evolve or even change as time passes but at the core of the organization's *raison d'être* lies its ability to reproduce them.

This comparison tells us about the fundamental differences between the project and the organization. It also confirms the value of the project for managers. For the project is a tool that they can use in their quest for what is, for them, the Holy Grail – the achievement of the organization's objectives. Projects can be used to create the changes that ensure the activities of the organization are carried out in a more efficient and more effective manner. They can even be used to redirect or even restructure the organization towards the goal of survival.

But, whatever its use might be, the project organization has to be compatible with its client. This remains true whether that client is an individual, a family, a small business or a corporate giant.

What sort of project organization?

How we organize our project is important.

Getting it right means that the management of our project has strong, firm foundations. These are the foundations upon which we can build to create the project and carry out its actions of **managing**, **planning**, **monitoring** and **controlling** – actions which support and reinforce our project's **doing**. If we get it wrong, then these actions are uncoordinated and uncooperative. Then our project will not only fail to provide us with the outcomes that we desire, it will also fail to do so within its defined boundaries of cost and time.

The ways in which we organize our project act to provide a co-ordinating framework within which these actions take place, as illustrated in Figure 3.1.

But what we do within the project isn't the only issue that this framework – the project organization – addresses. For, as we saw earlier in this chapter, the project has to be compatible with the structure, procedures and culture of its client. The key to achieving that compatibility also lies within the way in which the project is organized.

What we can now see is that our project's organization has two faces: that which turns inward – addressing its own internal actions and structure, and that which it presents to the outside world – to the project stakeholders, to the client organization. Both of these are important, but each of them must be kept in balance with the other.

For if we create a project organization that is dominated by the project's internal needs then, despite its efficiency, we will find ourselves out of touch with, adrift from, the needs and opinions of the stakeholders of our project. Similarly if we allow those stakeholder needs and opinions to dominate our project organization then we will find ourselves with a project organization that struggles to deliver a project outcome that is on time, to cost and functionally acceptable.

THE PROJECT ORGANIZATION FRAMEWORK

Figure 3.1   The project organization framework

Project aspects

When we make the decision about how to organize our project we must take into account a number of its aspects. The list starts with the obvious – the project's duration – but continues with the project's risk potential, importance to stakeholders, cost and complexity. All of these can influence our decision.

For example, a project for installation of a beverage vending machine has a well proven, low-risk outcome, doesn't involve new technology and has an estimated duration of days. This project will require an organization that is quite different from that of a project for the creation and launching of a manned rocket to Mars, which involves new technologies, a high risk outcome and extends over a period of years. Similarly, a project with a complex outcome, such as software for a new computer operating system, will need to be organized in ways that are different to the ways in which we organize a project for the purchase and installation of a home computer using Windows 98.

Whatever the nature of the project's organization might be, it must, ultimately, enable the project to be managed efficiently and effectively and to be completed to its planned duration, cost, performance and quality.

Project organizations

The spectrum of possible project organizations contains all the possible 'colours' and each of these has relevance for a particular type of project.

To help you choose the 'right' organization for your project we will look, first, at the two extremes of this spectrum and then at a third type of project organization that is often seen as a compromise between these extremes. As we do this we will look at the pros and cons and the demands and benefits of each of these types of project organization.

The Integrated project organization

This sort of project organization is a part of the client organization. It is, as far as possible, integrated into the line functions of that organization. The first thing to be decided is under which of these functions or divisions the project organization is to be located. This will depend upon both:

- the nature of the project outcome, and
- the nature of the client's organization.

For example, a project with an outcome of a production facility for a new product would be located in the Production Department while a project that aims to change quality standards and procedures will often, though not always, find a home in the Quality Department.

But what if there is no existing Quality Department or what if the Production Department is organized on a product basis, where then do we locate our project organization?

The answer can often be a compromise with the project organization reporting to a level of management that is senior enough to make sure that things get done but also has adequate relevant functional expertise.

When you use this sort of organization it means that:

- the project team consists of people who are a part of, employed by, the client organization
- these people can be used flexibly and in ways that reflect the size and priority of the project and their role in its team

- the project has easy access to the functional skills and experience of the client organization
- the same key experts are used by the project and the client organization
- the project and client organization procedures and systems are compatible, if not identical
- the project-end shift in ownership and responsibility is smooth and often hassle free
- the project team members are committed to the client organization and its objectives.

However, the disadvantages of this type of project organization are that:

- the client organization's priorities will lie with its day-to-day operations and this may limit the availability of key personnel and other project resources
- on 'influencing' projects, particularly those concerned with attitudes, the project is too close to the organization to effect real change
- most project team members will be part-time
- the motivation levels of project team members may be influenced by them seeing project duties as unimportant in the context of their individual ambitions and career plans
- the responsibility and authority of the project manager can be limited by an inadequate remit, organizational 'politics' or the quality and extent of his or her network connections within the client organization
- communications between the project and the client organization can often be informal and unstructured.

The Stand Alone project organization

This type of project organization stands completely free of and separate from the client organization. This means that it is self-contained and has its own resources, staff, premises, etc. On large projects it can have a structure and systems that are similar to those found in small companies.

When you use this sort of organization it means that:

- its team usually consists of full-time members
- these team members work directly for the project manager and are committed to the success of the project

- communications with that client organization are usually formal, regular and with a senior manager in that organization
- the project manager has full control over the project.

However, its disadvantages are that:

- duplication of staff roles can occur between projects
- project and client organization procedures and systems can be incompatible
- the skills developed and experience gained by project team members are lost when the project ends
- project teams can develop a 'tunnel vision' which ignores the needs and views of stakeholders
- project team members can be de-motivated by lack of job security or continuity.

The Matrix project organization

This sort of project organization can be seen as an attempt to combine the good points of both the Stand Alone and the Integrated organizations. Its structure is illustrated in Figure 3.2.

Figure 3.2   The structure of a Matrix project organization

It can also exist in a wide range of 'flavours' with the usual variation being the seniority of the line manager to whom the project manager reports. If this is low then the matrix is often described as being 'weak' and the project manager acts more as a co-ordinator than a manager. A minority of the project team members are full-time. In a 'strong' matrix the project manager reports to a senior line manager and acts with more independence and authority. Its team members are almost all full-time.

When you use a matrix organization it means that:

- the project can access resources, expertise and people from the client organization as and when required
- the project and client organization procedures and systems are compatible
- the project manager's authority depends on who she or he reports to
- the project team consists of people who are employed by the client organization.

But it has its disadvantages including that:

- project team members have two bosses – a functional boss and a project boss
- the balance of power, between the client organization and the project manager, can be precarious
- project shut-downs can be difficult
- conflict can arise from the fact that the decision-taking of project managers can be limited to administrative decisions while line managers take the technical decisions.

Your project organization

Before you decide what sort of organization you are going to use for your project, let's review what you already know – or should know – about the project.

It's worth writing this down on a piece of paper. Here are some headings that you can use:

- What is the project's outcome?
- What is its estimated cost?
- What is its estimated duration?
- Does the project involve new technology or significant risk?

Now we need to identify some of the more detailed stuff about your project and the relevant headings reflect that with questions such as:

- What tasks are involved in generating that outcome?
- What functional skills and abilities are required in order to achieve that outcome?
- What equipment is required in order to achieve that outcome?

Now you need to look at the client organization and ask yourself:

- Does it have the functional skills, abilities and equipment that the project requires?
- Will it be able to release them for use on the project?
- Does it have individuals with the project management skills and experience required?

Finally, ask yourself:

- What previous project experience does the client organization have?
- How were these projects organized?
- Which of them were successful?

By now, you should have all the information that you need to decide what sort of project organization you are going to have.

Let me give you a few pointers to start you on your way:

1. Large, long, costly projects usually need either Stand Alone project organization or strong Matrix organization so that the resources they need, to be managed effectively, are available when required.

2. If your client organization hasn't got the functional skills and abilities required to achieve the project outcome, or can't release them for the project, then you need a Stand Alone project organization that can effectively control, monitor and manage the subcontractors that you'll need to use.

3. If the project involves new technology then your choice of what organization to use must reflect whether your client organization has the feasibility study, prototyping and R&D (Research & Development) evaluation skills that will be needed. If it has, then use either an Integrated or a strong Matrix organization. If it hasn't, you'll have to subcontract

these and will probably need a Matrix or a Stand Alone project organization.

4 Small, short, low-cost projects can easily be handled by an Integrated project organization.

These pointers aren't intended as firm and hard 'golden rules' about the sort of organization that you choose. Your own experience and the experience of your client organization are just as important – as is, of course, your own judgement.

Project procedures and specifications

Whatever sort of project organization that you end up choosing, you have to make sure that the internal processes of the project are organized and conducted effectively and efficiently. The project will still need to be planned (see Chapter 4), managed (see Chapter 5), have cost estimates and budgets (see Chapter 7) and be monitored and controlled (see Chapter 8).

So that these actions can take place and contribute to the success of the project, we need to use good working practices to run our project. We can find examples of these in the international, national and industry specific standards such as PRINCE, PROMPT, RIBA's 'Plan of Work', Australia's HIA Quality Management and Systems, America's standards for Software Project Management (IEEE), Project Management (AIA) and Cost Engineering and Project Management (ANSI) and the British Standards Guide to Project Management (BS6079) and Use of Network Techniques in Project Management (BS6046). Further details of these can be accessed through the American National Standards Institution standards search site (see Further Information on page 161 for web address). You might also find them in the procedures and specifications of your workplace's Manual of Project Organization and Procedures. It's worth getting access to one of these – you may not want to use all of the procedures but they'll give you some useful pointers on how to do it well.

These documents will act as blueprints for the way in which the activities of our project ought to be conducted. As such they are generalized. What we need for our project is documentation that is specific to that project; documentation that tells us what our project is about and how it will be conducted. This is usually called a project manual.

So what do we need in our project manual? The simple answer is that it should contain the information that we, as project managers, need in order to manage the project. This means that, whatever the size, cost or nature of our project, we should have a source of information that tells us clearly and unambiguously about the Cost, Time and Performance aspects of our project and how we are going to manage, monitor and control those aspects. It doesn't have to be a massive tome – as you'll see shortly, it can be a few sheets of paper.

You should seriously consider including the following:

Project specification

This is a must for our project. It tells us what are the project's objectives, duration and sanctioned cost. For a short, low-cost project a single sheet of paper will be sufficient. A complex, high cost or long duration project will need something more substantial, often a separate volume of the project manual, with sections and appendices containing the detail of the project. This specification will have evolved as the project developed and may have been amended and rewritten several times. But once the project is given the go ahead, this specification should be frozen. From that point onwards, this specification should be subject to very little change or revision and any that does take place should be strictly controlled (see 'Project change control' below). As *the* definitive source of information about the project, it should contain the project's goals and objectives, scope, organization, budget and justification as well as telling us which techniques and systems we will use to plan, monitor and control the project.

Project roles and responsibilities

If our project is big enough to need a project team (see Chapter 6) then we need to know what the duties and responsibilities of each of the team members are. We also need to know what is expected of us when we carry out a particular role in that team. This information can be provided in the form of:

- Job descriptions
- Responsibility charts.

An effective job description should define:

- what the job should achieve
- what it needs to do to achieve that

- to what other position or job it is responsible
- what authority the job has in terms of decision making, hiring and firing, spending etc.
- what responsibility, if any, it has for client communications
- how its performance is measured.

Two sides of A4 paper are all you should need for this – any more than that indicates that you're not sure about what you want the job to do for you. If you're not sure about the objectives and responsibilities of the job, how can you expect the job holder to be?

A responsibility chart gives us a bird's eye view of who is responsible for what over the whole project. The level of detail shown should reflect both the size and complexity of the project as well as the needs of the project team. This is illustrated in Figure 3.3.

Project estimates and budgets

We look at the estimates and budgets of our project in more detail in Chapter 7. Both of these are important, though their uses are different. It's essential that your project manual identifies exactly what sum of money has been sanctioned and tells you what procedures will be used for expenditure approval and invoice payment and who is responsible for signing cheques etc.

Project change control

Despite the best of intentions, changes do happen, even on projects that are excellently managed. These can range from the substantial, as when new technology becomes available, to the small, as when detailed design work progresses and shows us a better way to do something. They can come about because of changes in legislation, or because of new technology, better designs etc. They can also come about because of mistakes and errors. Whatever their origin or size might be, all of these changes have the potential to alter the project's duration or cost or the nature and quality of its outcome.

It is essential that these changes are controlled. This means that, at the earliest possible opportunity, an effective change procedure must be established. This will require a clear, accessible and unambiguous statement of the project's 'base' line – as in the project specification mentioned above – and a process for the definition, evaluation and approval of any proposed changes to that specification.

TASK AREA	Project Manager	Mechanical Engineer	Civil Engineer	Electrical Engineer	Instrument Engineer	Process Design Engineer
Flowsheet design	◆	■		■	❖	●
Plant layout	◆	●	❖	■	■	■
Piping design	◆	●	■		❖	■
Instrumentation	◆			■	●	❖
Power supply	◆			●	■	

Key:
- ● Responsible
- ◆ Approval
- ■ Notified
- ❖ Support

Figure 3.3 Sample Responsibility Chart for an engineering project

A typical basic project change control form will contain:

- ■ an outline of proposed change
- ■ the reasons for the proposed change
- ■ which areas, costs, documents and drawings of the project are affected
- ■ who requested the change
- ■ who evaluated and approved/rejected the change.

Summary

Projects need to be organized and the selection of the 'right' project organization is a key step in the project's progress towards a successful completion. That organization needs to be compatible with the client organization and needs to provide a framework from within which the project's **doing**, **planning**, **monitoring** and **controlling** can be effectively carried out. The alternatives range from the Integrated organization to the Stand Alone organization with the Matrix organization in the middle ground. Choosing what is right for your project will involve you in finding out and understanding what has worked in the past, understanding the nature of the client organization's skills, experience and equipment, being aware of the project's outcomes, risks, costs, duration and special technology or knowledge needs – and in exercising your judgement as to what will work in the future. Whatever you choose, the first and essential step in organizing your project involves you in generating a project specification. You should also consider generating job descriptions, responsibility charts and budget, accounting and change control procedures.

4 | PLANS FOR YOUR PROJECT

A plan is an attempt to control the future. In this chapter we look at the value of planning to our project and the ways in which the project's future actions are ordered and sequenced to maximum effect. By the end of it you should have a better understanding of the steps and stages of the planning process and the tools that it uses.

Planning – now or never

When we look up the word 'plan' in the *Oxford English Dictionary* we are faced with a herd of alternative meanings.

A plan can be, amongst other things, a 'scheme for the economic development of a country', a 'drawing or diagram showing the relative positions of the parts of a building' or even, for John Wesley's early English Methodist Church, a 'periodic document listing the preachers for all the services throughout a circuit for the period'. These and other examples tell us that the plan is a versatile and commonly used commodity. The act of generating one – or planning – is something that many of us do.

That is, we all, at some time and in some way 'devise, contrive, design something to be done, or some action or proceeding to be carried out' (*OED*).

The results of all this planning are, of course, our attempts to control the future. However, things don't always work out in the ways we intend them to. As a result, we often have to face a reality that is different, in one way or another, to the one that we had planned. As somebody once said 'The future is not what it was.'

In our workplaces, the plans that we make are often challenged. The need for adaptability, the need to respond to customer needs, the tides of employee empowerment, decentralization, down-sizing and sweeping organizational re-engineering are just some of the things that act against our plans. Indeed, in today's workaday world many of the traditional management wisdoms, for whom planning and control were core issues, seem to have been challenged – and overthrown.

But is planning as out-of-date and old-fashioned as it seems – has it really been discarded in favour of today's instant responsiveness aided by ever faster computers? Or is it a powerful and flexible tool whose intelligent use we need to relearn in these volatile days?

The devil is, as always, in the detail and our answer lies not so much in the act of planning, but in the way that we *use* the plans that planning generates. For these are more than just lists of possible future actions. At their best, they are powerful visions of our hoped-for futures; our claims for immortality. But at their worst, they are unyielding, intractable expressions of the demands of others that suppress and choke our individual creativity and spontaneity. The difference between these lies not so much in the plan itself as in the ways in which we use it.

And therein lies the plan's deliverance. For as long as we need to reach out and try to shape and control our futures, then we will need to use the plan to help us achieve that end.

Projects and planning

The project and the plan are long-term bed mates. The project is a consciously chosen event and the plan is integral to its creation and completion. But the plan that we create must be resilient and adaptable if it is to be capable of withstanding the buffets and storms of our increasingly changeable workplaces. To cope it must be able to change – without losing sight of its endpoint – the project's outcome.

The act of planning is, in its essence, about the creation of a plan and that plan can take many forms. It can be a diagram, a table of figures, a programme of dates or a sequence of actions. But, whatever its form, it is a statement of our intentions regarding the future relationships of either a set of objects, as in an architectural plan of a building, or the times, places, etc. of our intended actions, as in our holiday plans.

For most of us, the plans that we create are about our future or intended actions. Our plan for a holiday might, for example, include the actions of obtaining visas, getting traveller's cheques, arranging for the cats to be fed while we are away, cancelling the deliveries of newspapers and milk and buying guides or maps for the areas in which we are going to travel.

But knowing what we intend to do isn't enough. We also need to know:

- when these actions are going to take place
- who is going to do them
- what resources are needed to do them.

Our holiday plan must tell us to apply, in good time, for our visas, to make sure we've enough money in our bank accounts when we buy our traveller's cheques and to make sure the neighbours or friends who usually feed our cats aren't away at the same time that we intend to be.

The plans of our projects have the same needs. They also need to know the **what**, **when**, **who** and **with what** of our actions if they are to enable us to shift their outcomes from desire to reality (see Figure 4.1). If we plan without attention to this detail then not only do we limit our ability to create our project outcomes at the cost, time and quality we desire, we may also limit our ability to create them at all.

THE PROJECT ORGANIZATION FRAMEWORK

Figure 4.1   Planning and the project process

THE ENGLISH PROJECT

Project goals and objectives: To make a cup of tea

Actions needed:
- check kettle water level and adjust as required
- switch on kettle
- get teapot
- get leaf tea
- get milk or slice of lemon
- get cup, saucer and jug
- put milk in jug or lemon on saucer
- allow kettle to boil
- switch off boiling kettle
- warm teapot by rinsing with hot water
- put leaf tea in teapot
- pour hot water into teapot
- leave to brew or infuse
- get strainer
- pour tea through strainer into cup
- add milk or lemon to tea

Duration: maximum of 10 minutes. **Actions by:** Phil Baguley

Equipment, tools and material needed:

Power point	Electric kettle,[1] lead and plug	Tea strainer
Cold water tap	Bottle of milk[2] in a refrigerator	
Teapot	Packet of leaf tea	Cup and saucer
Teaspoon	Jug for milk	

Notes: 1 Kettle suitable for gas stove is acceptable alternative
       2 Slice of lemon is acceptable alternative

Figure 4.2   The English Project – Objectives, Actions and Needs

The details of these future actions will, of course, be particular to the project that we are planning and are often contained in what is called a Work Breakdown Schedule (WBS) (see Chapter 7). A simple example, for a small domestic project that may be familiar to some of you, is given in Figure 4.2 on the previous page.

But the project's outcome, actions and duration aren't the only issues. We mustn't forget that our project has a budgeted cost and that a certain level of quality is needed in its outcomes. Both of these could affect either the way that we undertake the required actions or even the actions themselves. For example, in our English Project, the size of our budget will influence what sort of leaf tea we use and might even, if we have a restricted budget, persuade us to use a teabag rather than leaf tea. As a consequence of using this teabag we wouldn't need a teapot or a tea strainer and the sequence of actions that we followed would be different – as would the quality of the resultant tea. In summary, this cost factor can influence:

- the quantity of the project's outcome (a pot of tea or a cup of tea)
- the time taken to complete the project (teabag is quicker and less total time needed)
- outcome quality or fitness for purpose (does tea made from a teabag taste as good as tea made from leaf tea?)

Interdependency

The actions of a plan are always linked. Some of them, for example, cannot be started until other actions are finished – these are 'interdependent' activities, while other actions can be conducted at the same time – these are 'parallel' activities. When we look at our English Project, we find, for example, that the action of 'switch on kettle' should only take place after we've completed the action of 'check kettle water level and adjust as required'. Similarly the action of 'warm teapot by rinsing with hot water' can only follow the water in the kettle reaching boiling point and the action of 'switch off boiling kettle'.

See if you can spot any more relationships that are important, and then compare your answers with those given in Figure 4.3.

These relationships are important. Once we have found them, then the detail of the project's plan begins to emerge. We can then begin, for

ACTION NUMBER	MUST BE COMPLETED BEFORE OR AFTER ACTION No
1 Check kettle water level and adjust as necessary	Before 2
2 Switch on kettle	After 1
3 Get teapot	Before 10
4 Get leaf tea	Before 11
5 Get milk or sliced lemon	Before 7
6 Get cup, saucer and jug	Before 7
7 Put milk in jug or lemon on saucer	Before 16
8 Allow kettle to boil	After 2
9 Switch off boiling kettle	After 8
10 Warm teapot by rinsing with warm water	After 9
11 Put leaf tea in teapot	After 3, 4 & 10
12 Pour hot water into teapot	After 11
13 Leave to brew or infuse	After 12
14 Get strainer	After 12
15 Pour tea through strainer into cup	After 14 & 13
16 Add milk or lemon to taste	After 15

Figure 4.3   Action plan for the English Project

example, in our English Project, to ask questions like 'can we get the teapot, milk and cup and saucer while the kettle is boiling?' or alternatively 'can we get the milk and cup and saucer while the tea is infusing?' The answers will make a difference to not only the order in which we carry out our actions but also to the resources that we need to carry them out. But to be sure about that we also need to know how long each of these activities will take.

When we estimate the duration of these activities we can use a number of sources of information. For example, we can use measurements of the times taken for similar actions, we can get advice from others or we can draw on our own experience. For our English Project we can generate action times by using information from the kettle manufacturers (2 litres of water will boil in three minutes), the people who market the tea (To ensure full infusion use freshly boiled water and leave standing for five minutes), people who have done it before (friends, family or books) and our own experience (what did we do last time?). It's not necessary for these estimates to be absolutely accurate. For example, it will be enough, in our English Project, to be able to say how long the activities will take to within the nearest half minute. Remember that this is an initial estimate and that you'll have the opportunity later to refine this estimate, if you need to. On larger, longer and more complicated projects an accuracy of ± half a day will suffice at this stage in the planning process.

Whatever the accuracy of our estimates might be, the resulting plan needs to have certain characteristics. It needs to be clear, unambiguous and easily understood. It needs to contain enough detail to be meaningful and usable, but not so much detail that it becomes unnecessarily complicated. It also needs to be easy to change, update and revise as the timeline of the project progresses, so that we can monitor and record project progress. If our plan has all of these characteristics then it is not only usable, it is also a tool, an enabling mechanism that helps us to meet our goals.

A good plan will have all of these characteristics while a bad plan will be difficult to understand, awkward to use and contain inadequate or irrelevant detail.

Bars and charts

Most information is best presented in a visual form and the project plan is no exception.

One of the best and simplest ways of doing this is by the use of the Bar Chart or Gantt chart. This was developed around 1917 in America by an engineer called Henry L. Gantt. Despite its age, it has remained a popular method of presenting information about the project plan. The Gantt chart has a horizontal time scale, a vertical list of activities and a series of horizontal lines or bars with one for each activity. The length of each of these bars is proportional to the time needed to complete the activity that it represents.

A typical Gantt chart for a part of the English Project looks like the one in Figure 4.4. This shows us:

- when activities start and finish
- whether they have been completed

■ the project status at the point in time at which the chart was prepared

■ which activities are 'parallel' activities and can be done at the same time as others.

Activity description	Activity number	Minutes						
		1	2	3	4	5	6	7
Check kettle water level and adjust as required	1	[▅▅▅▅]						
Switch on kettle	2			[ ]				
Get teapot	3			[ ]				
Get leaf tea	4				[ ]			
Get milk or sliced lemon	5					[ ]		

Key: [Scheduled activity start
     ]   Scheduled activity finish
  ▬▬ Actual progress
    ◆   Current time

Figure 4.4   A typical Gantt chart

The Gantt chart can also show us the project's 'Critical Path'. This is the sequence, or pathway, of activities that determines the total project duration. If any of the activities on this pathway is delayed or extended then the completion time of the whole project is delayed. This pathway and the activities that make it up tell us which project activities we need to focus on to ensure that the project is completed on time.

Both the critical path and the 'same time' or parallel activities are shown on the full Gantt chart for the English Project (see page 55). When we look at this we can see that the project takes 11½ minutes to complete, compared with a target of 10 minutes, and that Activity 1 'Check kettle water level and adjust', Activity 2 'Switch on kettle', Activity 8 'Allow kettle to boil' and Activity 13 'Leave to brew or infuse' represent a major part of the Critical Path. If we were to reduce the kettle boil period by using a more powerful kettle or less water, then we would reduce the overall project duration. But this wouldn't be a reduction without limit as further inspection of the chart shows us that when we reduce the kettle boiling period from 3 minutes to 2½ minutes or less we change the Critical Path. Activities 3, 4, 5, 6 and 7 then replace Activity 8 on this path. However, the sequence of Activities 5, 6 and 7, which are about getting the milk or lemon ready for use – need not finish until the end of Activity 15 'Pour tea through strainer into cup', and could therefore take place parallel to Activity 13 'Leave to brew or infuse'. This would then enable us to reduce the duration of Activity 8 by a further 1½ minutes and reduce the overall project duration by a total of 2 minutes – from 11½ minutes to 9½ minutes.

The Gantt chart gives us a picture of the project that is clear and easily understood. Because of this it has remained one of the most popular forms of project plan, despite the more recent introduction of sophisticated and computerized network project planning systems. This popularity also reflects the fact that Gantt charts are easy to generate by hand – on standard graph paper or paper with pre-printed columns – and require limited training for their use. These characteristics make it particularly useful on small projects – in the home or the workplace. Proprietary versions of the wall mounted Gantt chart are available, having magnetic or special 'click in' strips, and are capable of displaying as many as one hundred activities.

But the Gantt chart does have its limitations, the major one being that it cannot easily or clearly show activity interdependencies. As we saw earlier, interdependency occurs when one activity cannot start until another preceding activity has finished. Knowing which activities are interdependent is important, if not essential, to the effectiveness of our plan and the efficiency of its resource usage. Indeed, when you think about it you'll realize that most critical paths are sequences of interdependent activities. The updating or revision of a large manually generated Gantt chart takes time and this can also cause problems, particularly at a time when that updated or revised plan is urgently needed. However, computer generated Gantt charts can help in that sort of situation.

Despite these limitations the Gantt chart does have significant advantages and is often used on small projects because of its low training demands and ease of generation, and on both large and small projects because of its direct and easily understood visual image.

Figure 4.5   The English Project Gantt chart

Networks

Network planning systems first became popular towards the end of the 1950s. The original systems were PERT (Programme Evaluation and Review Technique), which was aimed at working out whether a project would finish by a certain time, and CPM (Critical Path Method) or CPA (Critical Path Analysis), which was concerned with the trade-offs between the project's time and cost. Since that time their use has become very widespread and, not surprisingly, a number of other network systems have evolved, such as the Precedence Diagramming Method (PDM) or Activity on Node (AON) network, GERT (Graphical Evaluation and Review Technique) and VERT (Venture Evaluation and Review Technique). All of these have their particular uses and advantages (see Further Information section for relevant texts and web sites).

What we will do here, however, is to focus our attention on a simple and basic network planning system called the Activity on Arrow (AOA) network or Arrow Diagramming Method (ADM). This system of network planning is easy to understand and for small projects can be generated by hand or on a desk-top computer. AOA plans use a structured network to describe both the sequence of the project activities and the connections between those activities. Each of the activities is represented by an arrow and these are arranged so that they flow from left to right. Both the start and finish of an activity – or arrow – are marked by a circle – or node. These nodes are used, as we will see later, to store information about the duration of both the project and the activity.

Figure 4.6 shows a simple AOA network in which the activities are numbered 1, 2, 3, 4 and 5 and the nodes – which are also called events – are identified by the letters a, b, c, d, e and f.

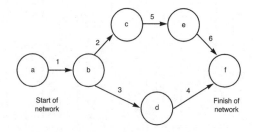

Figure 4.6   Simple AOA network

The rules for building these networks are simple and straightforward:

- the finish of one activity is also the start of the following activity – except at the end of the network
- activities can take place at the same time
- several activities can start from one event or merge into one event.

But, as it stands, this example network doesn't tell us about how long these activities take, whether any of them are interdependent or what the Critical Path is. To get to that point we need to know how long the activities take and what their dependencies are, as in Figure 4.7a.

Activity	Duration [hr]	Can only be completed after Activity
1	2	–
2	2.75	1
3	3.5	1
4	4	3
5	1	2
6	2	3 & 5

Figure 4.7a   Activity dependencies and durations

When we include this data in our network, it changes, as in Figure 4.7b.

Figure 4.7b   Simple AOA network with activity durations and dummy activity

The dotted line (called a dummy activity) tells us that Activity 6 cannot start until both Activities 3 *and* 5 are complete.

But this still doesn't give us all the information that we need. In order to get that we have to do some calculations. The results of these will tell us what is the earliest time that an event can take place, the 'earliest event time' or EET, and what is the latest time that an event can take place, the 'latest event time' or LET. To store this and other information in the network we have to change the circles – or nodes – to look like Figure 4.8.

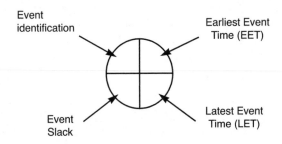

Figure 4.8 AOA network node

The data for the EET and the LET of each node are generated as follows:

- Start at the first event of the network and write the figure '0' in the EET location.
- Moving to event b, add the duration of activity 1 – which is 2 hrs – to the EET for event a – which is 0, giving a total of 2 hrs and write this in the EET location for event b.
- Follow through the network adding each activity duration to the previous EET and writing the resultant figure into the EET location of the relevant finish activity node.
- When you reach an event where two activities merge, as at e or f, write in the *highest* figure generated for the EET. Note that dummy activities have a zero duration.
- Continue to the last event and write the figure generated in *both* the EET and the LET locations of the last node.
- Starting from event f, trace the network backwards, subtracting the duration of the following activity from the LET at each event and writing the figure generated in the LET location in the node at the event's start.

■ When you reach an event at which two activities merge, as at d or b, write in the *lowest* LET calculated.

■ Continue this through to the first event – at which you should have an LET which is the same as the EET for this event. If you haven't, then you've made a mistake – probably at an event where two or more activities merge.

The figures we calculate will give us a network that looks like the one in Figure 4.9. Check your network against it.

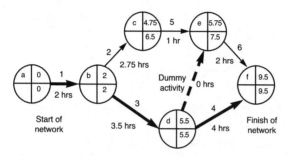

Figure 4.9   Calculating EET and LET

You'll notice that some of the arrows in this network are heavy and bold. These represent the sequence of activities that defines the overall project duration, i.e. the project critical path. You'll also be able to see – because event f has an EET and an LET that are both equal to 9.5 – that the project will take 9.5 hours to complete. But, if we look carefully, we will also see that activity 2 – which starts after 2 hours of project time – could finish at $2 + 2.75 = 4.75$ hours but doesn't need to finish until 6.5 hours. Similarly activity 5 could finish at $4.75 + 1 = 5.75$ hours but need not finish until 7.5 hours. These differences – between the time required and the time available for an activity – are called the 'float' or 'slack' of that activity.

This 'float' or 'slack' is useful to the ways that we schedule the project activities. For example, we could delay the start of the activity 5 until the LET (6.5 hours) of its start node or start at the original time – 4.75 hours – and extend the duration of the activity by using fewer people or a different method, up to a maximum of $7.5 - 4.75 = 2.75$ hours. In the full AOA network float is shown in the network nodes and the resulting network looks like Figure 4.10.

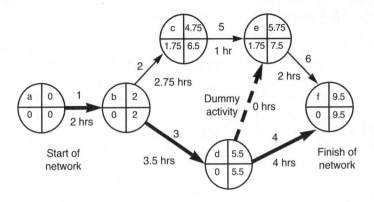

Figure 4.10   Full AOA network

So far we have assumed that we know, with certainty, how long our activities will take. But this isn't always so. We might, for example, be working with estimated durations whose values range from 'best' to 'worst' or from 'shortest' to 'longest'. When this happens we can calculate what is called an 'expected duration' for each activity and then use those to generate the network. To do this we use the following equation:

Expected activity duration $= \dfrac{(a + 4m + b)}{6}$

where   a   = estimated shortest activity duration
         b   = estimated longest activity duration
and   m = most likely activity duration.

Despite the fact that it has a lower level of visual impact than the Gantt chart, the Activity on Arrow network enables us to work out the results of network changes, as when, for example, an activity duration increases, without redrawing the network. This means that we can quickly examine the trade-offs between outcome, time, cost and quality. However, training and experience are needed if we are to make efficient and effective use of the AOA network. Despite this, the AOA network, in its computer-driven form, is often used on large and complex projects and is, without doubt, one of the most popular forms of project planning for this type of project. AOA networks can also be used, in the manually or computer generated form, for the small projects of our homes and workplaces.

Resources

So far, we have looked at two of the ways in which we can plan the project's use of time. But if we think about it we will soon realize that the Gantt chart and the AOA network both assume that the resources required for the project's activities are always available in the required quantity at the right time.

In reality, resource availability doesn't always reach that pinnacle of performance. The crane that we need might be in use elsewhere or the grade of paper we want might not be in stock. Some of these resourcing dilemmas might have their roots in the ways in which we plan. For example, as we saw in Chapter 1, the resource demands of the project can vary throughout its life cycle – with those of the Production phase often exceeding those of the other phases by several orders of magnitude. This might mean that we run out of booked mainframe computer time during this stage because we based our estimates on an average rate of usage. We may also have resourcing problems because we haven't taken into account the limitations that are built into the resources themselves or the task – such as the well known impossibility of getting ten men to dig, in one day, a hole which it would take one man ten days to complete.

In general, though, our resourcing difficulties come about because we are either short of time and need more resources to compensate, or because we don't have enough resources available, as when the promised delivery fails to materialize. What we need to do now is to look at how we can overcome these situations.

Activity slack

We saw earlier that we are able to regulate the way in which we complete an activity with slack or float by either delaying the start of the activity and using original resource level or by using the original start time and extending the activity duration by using fewer or different resources. This is called 'resource levelling'.

We can use it to smooth the project's pattern of resource usage. This means that there will be fewer (and smaller) peaks and troughs in that pattern. As we saw in our earlier English Project, this process of resource levelling for small projects is simple enough. The calculations involved can be done on a desk or pocket calculator – or even in your head! However, as the number of activities involved in the project increases, this process becomes more and more complicated. As a result, computers and specialized software are usually used for large or complex projects.

What did we do last time?

Sometimes we are faced with the need to decide what project activity we will use our scarce resource on. When this happens there often isn't enough time to undertake a reasoned and logical analysis. This is particularly true of the scarce resource allocation problems which are common in development projects, in which resource demand patterns are volatile and changeful. It would just take too long to look at all the options and choose the best solution. Under these circumstances we use heuristics or 'rules of thumb' to solve our problems.

These are rules that have, in the past, produced good results. They are also easy to understand and apply. Examples of the rules for our projects range from the obvious – 'Do critical path activities first' or 'Do activities with most subsequent critical path activities first' – to the less obvious – 'Do activities with smallest float first' and 'Do shortest activities first'. All of these represent simple and realistic solutions that can be applied quickly and cheaply to the resource problems that our projects generate.

Project planning with computers

There was a time – believe it or not! – when projects were planned without the help of computers.

Now, of course, things are different – we all own or have access to high powered desk top computers. There can be little doubt that they have completely changed the ways in which we plan our projects. But computer technology never stays still and we are always being offered new, better and faster computers and upgraded, modernized software packages to run on them. Because of this, any attempt to survey all of these and guide you towards what might be a 'best buy' for project planning would be not only foolish, it would be out of date before this book was published!

However, what this book will do is to identify some of the factors that you need to be clear about before you choose your project planning software package. This is an important step and it is often overlooked or given scant attention in the helter-skelter rush to buy the newest software.

Firstly, you need to think about your projects – about their size and complexity. Try, for example, to decide if they involve more than 500 activities or use multiple resources or if there is a high level of uncertainty about activity durations. Ask yourself if you'll need to keep people outside the project team informed about project progress and, if so, at what level of detail. Try to decide if you'll need to update the project plan frequently or to use resource smoothing or allocation. When you've got the answers to these questions then you're ready to move on to thinking about the sort of software that you need.

There are all sorts of project planning software packages on the market. Most, but not all of them, are designed to do just what you'd expect them to do – help you to plan your project. But the ways in which they do it are different and it's these differences that will lead you to buy one package or to reject another. The ease with which you can enter, model and schedule your project will be, for some of you, the critical factor in your choice. For others, it will be whether the package can handle costs or resources or a particular sort of report.

What you have to do is to identify the characteristics of the package that you want. Do you, for example, want it to be capable of generating AOA networks and Gantt charts or AON and Precedence diagram networks? Try to work out how many activities and nodes you want it to be able to handle and decide what sort of limitations you will accept in the way that these are identified. The range of calendar time that's built into the programme is important as can its ability to smooth or allocate resources, and handle costs and sub-projects.

High levels of user friendliness are vital – but you don't want to get lost in a maze of menus. The programme's outputs and reports must tell you and your clients what you both want to know. You'll need an understandable but comprehensive manual and software support – as and when *you* need it.

Finally, do make sure that the software you choose is compatible with your computer – its speed, hard disk capacity, RAM size and operating system version can be important.

Summary

The project plan is a mechanism that enables us to convert project objectives into concrete realities. To create that plan we need to know the **what**, **when**, **who** and **with what** of the project's actions as well as its budgeted cost and the level of quality needed in its outcomes. The plan can exist as a Gantt chart, an Activity on Arrow (AOA) network or an Activity on Node (AON) network. Each of these has its own set of advantages and disadvantages. Small projects often use Gantt charts or AOA networks while large or complex projects use AOA or AON networks. These projects use resources and these can be planned and managed by either resource levelling or heuristic rules. Finally we saw the importance of identifying our real needs before we choose the project planning software package we intend to use.

5 | MANAGING YOUR PROJECT

Managing a project isn't the easiest of tasks. In this chapter we take a look at the role of the project manager and the considerable influence that it has upon the success (or failure) of the project. By the end of the chapter you should have a better understanding of this role, the differences between it and the role of the day-to-day manager and the skills and abilities that the project manager needs to ensure that the project is successfully completed.

Management

Management is about organizing people and things so that they generate the results that we want.

The role of the manager is a very common one. We have presidents, prime ministers, archbishops, superintendents, football coaches, work group co-ordinators, office managers, baseball team managers, restaurant managers and rail station supervisors – and these are all managers. But what, if anything, do they have in common?

To find an answer to that question we have to first recognize that the manager is a creature of our organizations. These, as we saw in Chapter 3, have structures, with roles and responsibilities. The manager is one of the most important of these roles. He or she has a formal authority over the whole or part of the organization. This gives him or her, power, status and access to information and resources. But these are not unconditional gifts. For the organization expects that the manager will only use these to achieve its objectives – whatever these might be. The people who act as managers are selected and appointed – a process that assesses an individual's abilities and skills and compares them to those thought to be needed to do the job. The formality and visibility of this process can vary: in some organizations it is a 'behind closed doors' process, while in others it is a very public and open process in which all stakeholders are involved.

There are many views about what a manager does. However, the majority of them seem to agree that the manager acts in ways that:

- ■ display leadership and have authority
- ■ monitor and disseminate information
- ■ take decisions and resolve conflicts.

Managing projects vs day-to-day management

We have already seen the Five Fundamentals of the project – its one-off nature, its limited and defined time span, its uniqueness, its defined outcome and its focus on change. The organization is different. As we saw in Chapter 3, its prime concern lies in survival and in ensuring that it can continue to produce – repeatedly and accurately – replicas or hybrids of its products or services. These differences begin to give us clues about the different ways in which the project and the organization need to be managed.

Organizations are primarily concerned with stability, continuity and repetition. Their day-to-day operations take in customers or materials and process or service them in ways that are routine and often fixed. The resources – equipment, buildings – that are used in these operations are also fixed and static to ensure their consistent availability. The managers of these operations are concerned with continuity and consistency and satisfying the often conflicting needs of the task, the organization, the customer and his or her staff. This is done by trade-offs between the factors of cost, time, output and even quality.

In contrast, the management of our projects is concerned with creating and sustaining change. Resources come and go, as required. The project manager has little freedom to exercise trade-offs – because her or his project has a fixed, finite, limited time scale, cost and outcome. As a consequence, her or his skill and judgement are exercised in ways that are far more focused. On the average project there are few opportunities to reverse out of your mistakes.

Most day-to-day managers are functional specialists. They are engineers, production managers, accountants, nursing managers, sales managers, marketers, designers, bankers or personal finance specialists. As such they manage departments, sections and groups dedicated to those functions.

The project manager, however, is a generalist, a facilitator, an enabler. The project manager rarely has in-depth specialist knowledge; she or he oversees specialists and facilitates the contributions that their expertise make to the project.

The significance of all of these differences is such that project management is about the management *of* exceptions rather than *by* them. We might almost say that the effective project manager surfs the waves of change while the day-to-day manager stays at anchor in the relative calm of the harbour. Of course, both have their places in our world but the ways in which they operate are very different. Because of these differences, projects must be organized, planned and managed in ways that differ from those that we use in our day-to-day activities – as we will see in the chapters that follow.

Projects and managers

Managers and projects come together either because the manager takes over and manages the completed project's outcome or because she or he is responsible for the management of the project itself.

It's the second of those roles – that of the project manager – that we will look at now.

The project is the most effective way of creating change. Managing it well demands a diverse and unique set of skills and experience. The project manager needs to be a broad view generalist, able to integrate or bring things together – creating, for example, a whole project from its disparate parts. To be effective the project manager must be:

- familiar with and able to use project management tools and techniques
- able to make sure that the project's money is spent in ways that maximize its benefit to the project
- skilled in fostering co-operative working relationships within the project team and with all the project stakeholders
- able to identify risks and act in ways to limit their effects upon the project.

This is a demanding and stressful role. It's said that the only comfortable and relaxed project manager is one who is either waiting for her or his next project or one who is on the edge of failure in their current one. It is, nevertheless, a role which exerts significant influence upon both the direction of and the potential for success of the project.

In order to do this the project manager must be able to:

- **lead** – a team of skilled individuals
- **communicate** – with everyone who is involved in the project
- **motivate** – the project team, contractors and sub-contractors
- **negotiate** – effective solutions to the conflicts that arise between the needs of the project and its stakeholders.

These skills are needed whether our project is large or small, to do with our workplace or our home, and worth a small fortune or a pittance.

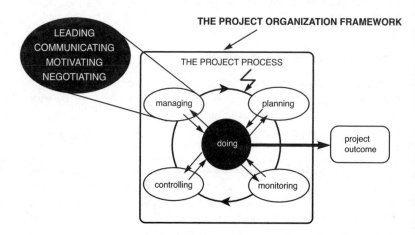

Figure 5.1   Managing and the project process

Leaders and leadership

Somebody once said that leadership is about persuading people to do what they should have done in the first place. It's also about the ways in which we influence the thoughts and actions of others.

This can come about because of our role in an organization, as sales supervisor, production manager or CEO, or because of our personality, as in the 'charisma' that we possess. In each of these situations we exert influence on others, either because of the authority given to our role or because we behave in ways or say things that attract them or that they wish to emulate.

But these aren't the only ways by which we can influence people. We can also influence what people do or say because:

- we are able to punish them if they act in ways other than those that we approve of or desire,
- we are an expert in a certain field,
- we are able to grant (or withhold) benefits or things they desire,
- we have access to others who might also do all or any of the above.

By now you've probably spotted that other people than leaders can do some of these. A manager, for example, can sack you or give you a raise or a supervisor can be an expert in welding or word processing.

But being a manager or a supervisor isn't the same thing as being a leader. A manager is about forecasting, planning, organizing, commanding, co-ordinating and controlling, whereas being a leader is about something else. The leaders are people who exert a directing influence or guidance; they can do this about spiritual, political, national or commercial matters. They inspire us by creating visions of desired futures. We also know that there are far more managers than leaders. Indeed, a true leader – one who creates such a response in us such that we, literally, would follow him or her – is a very rare bird.

But when we think about this we will soon realize that being a manager and being a leader aren't mutually exclusive – we can manage and we can also lead. But being one doesn't automatically mean that you are or can be the other. Being good at leading doesn't necessarily mean that you are good at managing, or vice versa. Perhaps the right way, for most of us, is a combination of the two – the ability to influence backed up by the ability to plan, organize, co-ordinate and control.

So, then, given that most of us know how to manage, how can we become more of a leader ?

There was a time when the answer to this question would have been that you can't *become* a leader – you either are one or you aren't. This view – that leaders are born and not made – was popular for a long time. But years of dedicated research by many people failed to come up with an adequate answer to what it is in your background or genetics that makes you a leader. Bearing this in mind and remembering our starting point – that leading others is about influencing them – we begin to see that leadership is not as simple and straightforward as some would have us believe. The textbooks of management contain many, many views of the ways that leading is, or ought to be, carried out. While the good thing about all this is that it gets us away from the 'leaders are born' school of thought, the bad thing is that it can be confusing. However, there does seem to be a consensus that what is appropriate – in leadership terms – depends upon a number of things. Amongst the more significant of these we find such things as:

- the location in which the leadership is being applied
- the culture of the organization
- what the task is or what's being done
- how the followers like to be led.

All of this means that there isn't a single unique style of leadership that will always produce the best results. As they say, it all depends.

When we think about this it begins to make sense. We know (or can imagine) that the style of leadership that is appropriate to a battlefield situation is different from that used in the 'work-a-day' office situation. The leadership style that works when a team is doing a routine task is different from the one needed when the team task demands high levels of creativity. Effective leadership takes into account and answers the needs of both the task in hand and the group working on that task.

Because our projects are one-off unique events, this means that there is no single 'right' style of project leadership. Instead, there is a range of different styles, some of which will work with certain projects and project teams and not work with others.

An effective project team leader takes into account the nature of the project, the prior experience and composition of the project team and the project's time, money, and quality constraints. Large projects mean big teams. These need to be organized in ways that are different from the ways that we organize the teams of small projects. Experienced project teams will need less direction than inexperienced ones and teams who have worked together before may (or may not!) work together better than teams of strangers. The projects of our homes demand leadership that is different from the projects of our workplaces.

In the end, effective project leadership is about getting the required results as and when they are needed. If the project manager is going to achieve that then she or he must be able and willing to communicate with the people involved in that project – and this we will now look at.

Project managers and communication

The boardroom and the bedroom are two of the places that shout for effective communication. But they're not the only ones. Communication is key to all of our lives. We need to 'get our message across' to everyone – work colleagues, partners, customers, children, parents, teachers and doctors. But in some of the roles that we carry out, effective communication is *the* primary skill.

One of these is the role of the project manager. Project managers spend a lot of their time communicating. They do it with almost everyone involved in the project. The list is almost endless – client managers, contractors, project team members, union officials, government inspectors. All of these and others have to be listened to, explained to, informed, sold ideas and persuaded.

Communication has, at its core, the act of exchanging information. A rich and complex two-way process with an interplay of message and reply, of input and feedback, it uses both the written word, as in letters, memos and reports, and the spoken word, as when we speak to each other face to face or over the telephone. We also inform each other through our gestures, movements, expressions, postures and gaze.

Project communications

The communications that take place in our projects are important. They enable us to exchange facts, broker information, exert influence and even, on occasions, to express emotions. They are both formal and informal in nature.

The formal communications of the project are targeted at answering the information needs of the project stakeholders. As such they should be planned with care and precision. That planning should identify who needs what, when it's needed and what form it's needed in. Issues such as the immediacy of information needs – as in e-mail or snail mail – and the technology involved – as in Internet or Intranet – should be debated and resolved. These formal communications should be about the project performance. As such, they should give the project stakeholders information about:

- what work has been done since the last communication
- what work should have been done in that period
- what work is planned for the next period.

They should also provide up-to-date information on the cost performance of the project such as the budgeted and actual spend to date, the budgeted spend to completion etc. This information can be expressed as bar charts (see Chapter 4), S curves (see Chapter 8), schedule and cost variance reports or Earned Value reports (see Chapter 8). The formal communications of the project can take place in meetings or be generated in hard copy or electronic form. Meetings are held to review project progress and can be actual or video conferenced. Which you choose will depend upon the size of the project and the availability of networked information systems.

The informal communications of the project are just as important as the formal ones, but they are often underrated or taken for granted. They take place in the innumerable casual conversations, telephone calls, chats and discussions that litter our days. They are accidental, unplanned, fortuitous and spontaneous. They are, however, the ways and means of most of our communications. The ways in which they are used by the project manager can be crucial to the success of the project. The project manager is not wasting her or his time when she or he visits, in the early days of the project, everybody who has anything to do with the project. She or he is laying down the framework of an informal communications network that will, in future days, be crucial to the success of the project.

Skill in the 'art' of communication is a must for all project managers. They all, if they are to be effective, must be able to write, speak, listen to and read body, spoken and written language with skill and ability. Effective communication can make a considerable contribution to the success of the project.

Project managers and negotiation

We are all negotiators. We learn to do it 'at our mother's knee'. We continue to use and develop our negotiating skills throughout the rest of our lives. The things that we negotiate about reflect every aspect of our lives and these negotiations take place everywhere we work and play.

The project manager is no exception to this. His or her negotiations are about every aspect of the project. They can be structured and formal – resulting in written agreements – or informal and about generating verbal understandings. All of these negotiations take place because of the conflict that occurs when the drives that we all have, to achieve goals that answer our needs, are frustrated. When this happens, strife and argument arise. Then, we need to find a way forward. For if we fail to resolve these conflicts they will divert the energy and drive of the project team away from what should be its primary objective – achieving the project's goals. The key lies in the art of negotiation.

Negotiating and bargaining

When we negotiate with someone we become involved in a search. It's a search to find, firstly, general areas of agreement and acceptability and then, secondly, to identify specific outcomes that are acceptable.

But this is not a search that we conduct on our own – the outcomes that we generate must, if they are to work, be *mutually* acceptable. For not only are they the solutions to today's problems – they also define the ways in which we will interact in the future. Bargaining is an important part of this process. It involves us in haggling, dealing or bartering – acts with which we are all familiar.

The negotiations of our project can be about anything to do with that project. In its early stages they can be about such issues as the project's objectives or its organization. In later stages, plans, schedules and procedures, contracts, prices and priorities can be involved. By the end of the project they can be concerned with the detail of the project handover and the subsequent list of items needing corrective action.

The manner in which these negotiations are conducted and the quality of their outcomes are important. Negotiations with win–win endings have an influence beyond the bargaining table. They create an environment with a genuine shared will to succeed. This sort of negotiation starts by identifying areas of potential agreement.

Ways and means

In its simplest form, negotiating involves two people. It is a face to face debate on some matter of shared interest. Its outcome is a mutually acceptable settlement or compromise.

Let's, for the moment, imagine that two people – A and B – are negotiating about the sale of some land. A would like to sell the land and B wants to buy it. Their shared objective is to try to find out if they can agree on a price. But as we watch them we begin to realize that there isn't just one price involved. B, for example, will have one price which she or he is not prepared to exceed and another, lower, price that she or he hopes to buy at. A will also have two prices: the one below which she or he is not prepared to sell and the another, higher one, which she or he hopes to sell for. But neither knows what the other's prices are and they open the process of negotiation with the first of a series of offers and counter offers. B will offer to buy at a very low cost and A will reject that, countering with a very high offer to sell. The levels of these offers are chosen so that they can be changed and, in so doing, appear to be offering compromise. This process of offer–counter offer will continue with B attempting to pull down A's price offer, if possible to his or her 'hoped for' cost, while A will attempt to push B's offers up, again, if possible to the level of his or her 'hoped for' price. These prices lie in a spectrum of value which looks like Figure 5.2.

Rising Value

Seller's initial offer
Seller's desired price
Maximum buyer cost
Minimum seller price
Buyer's hoped for cost
Buyer's initial offer

Figure 5.2   Value spectrum

When we watch the tactics and games that are used during this offer–counter offer sequence we might see A giving ground slowly and reluctantly in response to B's threats of withdrawal. These threats might be countered by A invoking things like other offers, company policy or saying that there is nothing left to give. The final position that is reached in this game of push and pull will depend upon how skilled and experienced the negotiators are, whether there are alternative sellers or buyers and what prices had been agreed in other, similar, negotiations. If it's a win–lose negotiation, rather than a win–win one, then you can also add the incentive created by whoever lost last time not wishing to repeat the experience.

In most negotiations A and B would, by now, have entered what is often called the **bargaining zone**. The upper boundary of this zone is the maximum price that B (the buyer) is prepared to pay and its lower boundary is the minimum price that A (the seller) is prepared to accept. Obviously, if B's maximum is less than A's minimum, then the zone will not exist and the negotiation will fail. For A and B to enter this zone and achieve a successful win–win conclusion to their negotiation requires real skill and commitment on both their parts. They will need to be able to create a relationship which is built on mutual trust. In order to do that they must be able to identify not only what is happening but also why it is happening and what needs to be done about it. They will also need to be able to communicate with each other with clarity and precision and listen without bias or prejudice.

The project manager is involved in negotiations at every stage of the project's life cycle and the way in which she or he negotiates can make a considerable difference to the success of the project.

Project managers and motivation

Motivation is what gives our behaviour direction and purpose.

When we are motivated to do something – or 'turned on' to it – it is usually because it leads to us getting something that we want. Motivation is a complex process and the question of what motivates people to perform effectively is not an easy one to answer.

One of the more accessible views about this was that of Abraham Maslow. His view was that human beings are in a state of incessant need. For almost all of us, these needs are only partially satisfied. It is this state of unsatisfaction that drives us to act in the ways that we do. Maslow suggested that these needs, which he classified into five basic groups, are arranged or 'stacked', one above another, as on a staircase. On the first step of this staircase are our physical needs – for food, warmth and shelter. These are followed by our needs for protection and security and then our affection and attachment needs. Towards the top of the staircase are our needs for reputation and recognition. Finally, at the top, is our need for self-fulfilment. These need groups are said to act upon us in their order on the 'staircase' and are at their most potent when they are unsatisfied. For example, we have to satisfy our basic need for warmth, food, water and shelter before we begin to seek 'higher' needs such as job security, prestige and the freedom to create. However, this is not a totally rigid staircase and there are, as Maslow pointed out to us, people for whom self-esteem is more important than love or for whom the fulfilment of their creative needs overrides all other needs.

So, can we apply this view of motivation to our projects? The answer is yes, but a conditional yes. We need to be aware that people are not as simple or as straightforward as this theory appears to suggest. The enormous complexity shown by people every day challenges the apparent simplicity of this 'staircase' of needs. But, it does, nevertheless, provide us with some useful information. It tells us, for example, that people come to work for other needs than the money with which to answer their basic needs of food, warmth, shelter and security. They need, for example, to answer their social and their creative needs as well.

The project manager who ignores these other 'higher' needs does so at his or her peril. A not-so-old saying confirms this when it tells us to 'find the right people and then get to hell out of their way'. A wise project manager recognizes and allows for the fact that people need to plan and control their own work and need to be involved in management decisions about that work.

Key people on the project manager's list of people to be motivated are the members of the project team. Teams are unusual and we will explore them in more detail in the next chapter. For the time being we need to note that team members can be motivated to perform better by either enlarging or enriching their jobs.

Role enlargement involves extending a role's duties or responsibilities. It happens, for example, when we ask the project electrical engineer to take on the responsibility for the project computers. Role enrichment, however, involves allocating more interesting or challenging duties to a role. It happens when we ask that electrical engineer to be responsible for decisions about major project contracts that are concerned with other than electrical engineering.

Motivating the project team, however it is achieved, is a key task for all project managers. It remains a simple but powerful truth that well-motivated project staff perform well and in so doing contribute to the success of the project.

Summary

Management – organizing people and things so that they produce the results that we want – is a very common act and the manager is one of the most important of the roles of all our organizations. Managers are selected and appointed and are given formal authority over part or all of the organization, as well as status and access to information and resources. Most of the many views about what a manager does tell us that she or he acts in ways that display leadership and authority, monitors and disseminates information and takes decisions and resolves conflicts.

The job of the project manager is different from the job of the manager who is concerned with day-to-day operations. She or he uses resources that are transient, rather than fixed, and on a time scale that is frozen, rather than indefinite. The project outcome is unique, rather than a replication, and the project manager is primarily concerned with creation of change. She or he needs to be a gifted, broad view, generalist who can integrate or bring things together. The effective project manager is a key factor in the success of a project. She or he needs to have and be able to use a wide range of competencies including: the ability to lead a team of skilled individuals, communicate with everyone who is involved in the project, motivate the project team, contractors and sub-contractors, and negotiate effective solutions to the conflicts that arise between the needs of the project and its stakeholders.

6 | YOUR PROJECT TEAM

Team is both a word and an idea. It's one that is well-known to most of us. This chapter looks at teams – the ways in which they do (and don't) work and the ways and means of their operation. By its end you'll understand more about the nature of the team, what it can (and can't) do, the factors that influence its performance and the considerable potential of its contribution to the project.

Why teams?

The team – or rather the team that *works* – gives us a way of working together that is both versatile and effective.

In all sorts of situations – at work, at play, and in the home – the team has a proven track-record of creativity and achievement. Most of us have experienced, at some point in our lives, that extra 'something' that a good team can create. A team that works well can, sometimes literally, 'move mountains'. The team takes our individual efforts and synergizes them into a greater whole. It is capable of growing, changing and adapting to meet new demands. The team is able to survive and even reinvent itself as, and when, individual members move on or its original task changes.

But experience also tells us that the team can be a difficult place to work in. For being a team member means that we have to give up some of our individuality to submerge ourselves in a greater whole. It can also expose us to feedback about ourselves and our job performance that can be uncomfortable.

So why does the team exist and why do we use it? The answer is a simple one. Teams exist because they have the potential to outperform our individual efforts. Their performance also surpasses those of all the other sorts of social groups that exist in our organizations. Put simply, there is nothing to beat a good team – either in terms of its performance or our experience of it !

It is this potential that is important to our projects. It can convert a moribund, mediocre project into a thriving, sparkling success. In this chapter we will look at what it is that gives a 'good' team that potential and how we can use it in the process of managing successful projects.

What is a team?

The word 'team' is, of course, a very common one. It's used on our sports fields, as in football, soccer, rugby, baseball and basketball teams, and in our workplaces, as in 'Finishing shop team' or 'Telephone sales team'. When we look it up in the dictionary we find the word 'team' is defined by phrases like 'a number of people' and verbs such as 'collaborating' and 'working together'. Teams generally have members with defined functional roles, such as 'goalkeeper', 'pitcher' or 'team leader', and what goes on inside them is often seen to be co-operative and constructive, as in 'team spirit' or 'team work'.

But isn't this the same as a group? The answer is no, it isn't. The word 'group' – which is defined as 'an assemblage of persons' who are 'standing together' – is used to describe a number of people with a purpose or interest in common. Examples are a group of baseball fans or a group of theatre-goers. The team – which also consists of people – is different. Its members have a purpose that is generated by consensus and debate. Because of that, the purpose is shared by the team. People in groups act as individuals, following their own individual desires and needs. Team members act together in ways that are co-operative and aimed at generating outcomes that are desired by the whole team rather than any one individual. The outcomes that teams generate are often definable, even measurable 'products' – such as a design for a new car or a completed project. Group outcomes are much more diffuse and generalized – such as 'influence' or 'power'.

The groups of our workplace have a strong functional flavour, as in the Marketing or the Accounts Department, and their composition and size reflect the demands of that function. They also almost always have leaders – a role that remains with a single individual who is formally appointed. Their meetings are formal, structured, orderly events that delegate work to others outside the meeting.

Our teams, however, are task focused. Their leadership is less formal – even to the point of being shared – with the leader role moving around the team as the availability of individuals or the phase of task in hand changes. Their meetings are usually open-ended, untidy debates aimed at solving problems.

All of this tells us that it's the team – rather than the group – that we want in our projects. For the team provides us with a way to tap into and harness the efforts, skills, abilities and creativity of all who are involved. This is true for all our projects – at work, at home or at play. The team has a considerable potential to contribute to their success.

However, teams don't always succeed and what we now need to begin to look at is what it takes to create and manage a 'good' team.

Good teams and bad teams

First, the bad news: the team, despite its considerable potential, doesn't always walk on water.

There are times and places when it doesn't work. This often happens when it's misapplied or used inappropriately, resulting in disruption and a waste of time and money. It can also be badly managed so that the initiative and creativity of individual team members are suppressed, inhibited or even overwhelmed. A team can lose touch with reality, creating its own set of values and ways of seeing the world, leading to outcomes that are not compatible with or desired by the real world outside.

But, despite all of these risks, the team is here to stay. This is because, at its best, the team is one of the most flexible and productive mechanisms for empowering and enabling of people. It produces results that are not only desired by our organizations – they are essential to their survival. The team and performance go together like sugar and spice – different, but an unbeatable combination.

So, how do we create and manage a 'good' team? The answer to this question is, as usual, a mixture. In this case, the ingredients are common-sense and best practice. Our workplace teams exist within our organizations. As such they are influenced by the values, culture and 'ethos' of those organizations. These can act on the teams in different ways. They can encourage and support them – or they can limit their performance. For example, an organization that values performance, even above other values or standards, will be one in which teams will work well. It's the need for performance that counts – the team is the means rather than the end. But performance on its own is not enough – it has to be meaningful performance, performance that the team considers to be important. That organization also has to be one in which individualism is prized but not at the expense of team membership. A 'good' team will not reject our individual creativity. It will find ways and means of accepting and using them. Nor will a good team operate in isolation. It will act and interact in ways that answer the needs of those around it.

In order to do that it has to have the 'right' size and the 'right' mix of team members.

How many

Size is an important aspect of team operation. Get it wrong and you'll limit the effectiveness of the team. Too big a team means that its members won't just have trouble in communicating effectively with each other, they'll also have difficulty in taking decisions and solving problems in ways that tap into, or make use of, the skills and knowledge of all the team members. Too small a team and you'll find yourself short on skills, expertise and people-time, despite the fact that you can communicate easily with each other.

So what is the 'right' number? The pragmatic answer is that it – the 'right' number for *your* team – lies within a range of sizes. What decides the size of your project team are factors such as the demands of the project task, the availability of the 'right' people and the sort of project organization that you've chosen.

Here are some guide lines.

Best practice seems to indicate that if you go above twenty-five members, then you're not talking about a team any more. But if you go below three members, then you'll run the risk of running short of relevant skills and experience and people-time. In general, the consensus seems to be that it's worthwhile limiting your team size to ten people.

But even that isn't a 'golden' number – to be applied whatever the team's task is. For example, for tasks in which member participation and involvement are key issues, such as joint union/management study groups, the evidence is that the team size should be limited to between five and seven members. Other studies of teams indicate that, if we want to harness the efforts, skills, abilities and creativity of our team members, then we have to limit the size of the team to between six and eight people.

This may mean that, on large projects or projects with high staffing levels, we need to organize ourselves so that we have a series of interconnected teams with main team members chairing or leading the satellite teams and taking responsibility for the smooth and easy flow of information between the main and satellite teams, as illustrated in Figure 6.1.

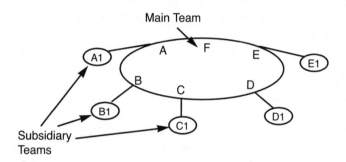

Figure 6.1   Main and satellite teams

Getting the size of the team right is not, however, the only factor. We also have to make sure that we have the right mix of people.

Who – and Why

We all work in different ways. Some of us are analytical, logical, careful and considered in the ways that we work. We make our decisions with care and after due consideration of all the facts. Others make decisions quickly, almost impulsively, relying upon instinct or 'gut feelings'. But neither of these, nor the many other ways of taking decisions, are 'right'. More importantly, none of them are 'wrong'. They are simply different from each other.

But the differences between us aren't just about the ways in which we take decisions. We behave in different ways, have different values, believe in different things, have different likes and dislikes and communicate in different ways. Some of these are compatible with each other and some are not.

All of this diversity means that the job of selecting the 'right people' for your team is important. Get it wrong and you'll have conflicts, difficulties and a poor team performance; get it right and you'll still have conflicts and difficulties but you'll also have a team that works.

Having said all of that, I'm also aware that some of you may not have the freedom to choose your own teams. You may have inherited them from a previous project manager or may have been given a team chosen by those above you in your organization. Your project team may consist of members of your family or a few willing volunteers. In these circumstances it's important that you take time out from the business of the project to find ways of working together. If you've inherited a team, there may be resentment about your 'taking over' from or even 'usurping' the previous team leader. It's important that you face that early and get the team to recognize that you need them – and they need you.

Unfortunately the news that teams need to be selected carefully, and as a whole, hasn't reached everywhere. Many of our organizations select their teams using the criteria of functional skill only. This ignores the person behind that functional skill. In other situations people get chosen for teams because they are easy to get on with, do what they are told, don't rock the boat etc., etc. This, of course, ignores the issues of functional skill and creativity.

If we are to choose a successful team then we need to use some basic and relevant entry criteria. Of course, team members need to have the required functional skills. But they also need to have demonstrated their ability to work co-operatively with others when making decisions or solving problems and be willing to give up part of their own 'ego-space' in order to become integrated in the team. This task of integration into the team is not an easy one. One way of overcoming its difficulties is to pick people as team members because of all the above *plus* their ability to carry out at least one of the roles that a balanced team needs. These are generally about things like coming up with new ideas, defusing conflict or tension, looking after the team chores, analysing what's happening or even challenging the position of the rest of the team. If you think about it you'll soon realize that 'good' teams have all these roles and, as a result, can operate in ways that are independent of individual efforts or skills.

Finding out whether potential team members are up to these sorts of role, as well as meeting the basic entry criteria that we identified earlier, isn't an easy task. But, there is a surprising amount of information about. You can find out, for example, how they've performed in other teams, what their attitudes and responses have been to relevant training and development programmes or what their current or ex-bosses think about their team skills. You can also use one of the commercial team role assessment questionnaires that are available.

The task of selecting a team is key to its success. With the right mixture of complementary skills, abilities and experience, the team has a potential that exceeds, by orders of magnitude, the sum of the abilities and skills of its individual members.

The Team Charter

Once your team is selected – either by chance, circumstance, yourself or others – then it's time for you, the team leader, to bring them together.

But this first meeting isn't just a social, 'getting-to-know-you', event. It's a beginning of the process by which this collection of individuals will evolve, change and develop into an effective, working, results-generating team. It may also be the first time that you meet them in your role of team leader. There should be no exemptions from this meeting – it's a must-be-there meeting for all the team members and should be scheduled and arranged in ways that recognize that.

The primary purpose of this meeting is the generation, discussion and agreement of the Team Charter.

This isn't a legal contract or agreement. In fact, for some teams it won't even exist on paper. But it is important because it identifies the why, what, when and how of the team. It will provide the answers to the obvious questions of 'What are we going to do?', 'How long will it take?' and 'Who are our customers?'It will also answer the more subtle – but just as important, questions such as 'How are we going to work together?', 'Will we all be involved in key decisions?' and 'What principles are important to us as a team?' The answers to these and other questions make up the Team Charter. They need to be hammered out in this first meeting. It does help if you, as team leader, have thought through where you stand on the key issues and prepared a draft document for discussion. This should tell the team about:

- its task
  - what, by when, at what cost, etc.
- the key customers
  - names, roles, expectations
- the project stakeholders
  - names, expectations, conflicts.

It should also give them some idea of the options for:

- how communications are to be managed
  - with customers and stakeholders and between team members
- how team performance will be measured
  - key results, milestones, outcomes
- what procedures and rules will be used
  - must-be-done rules, areas of discretion
- how the team will work together
  - principles of team operations.

Remember that this is a draft and try and get the level of detail right. Too much and people will feel that any real discussion has been pre-empted; too little and the discussions will produce nothing more than a series of 'broad-brush' generalities. It's worth starting off with a package of statements which define, irrespective of the detail level of your draft, the core principles of the way in which you want the team to operate. Good examples would be:

- Working together is more productive than working apart.
- Joint decisions are stronger than solo ones.
- Team meetings are jointly owned.

In the end, the content, detail, form and structure of your team charter is down to you and your team. But if it's going to work then it must provide urgency and direction to the team's efforts as well as being a means of focusing the creativity and energy of all team members.

Team building

We've already seen that the first team meeting is important – if not vital – to the creation of the team charter. But that's not all that happens there – it's also the beginning of the team building process.

Teams don't just spring spontaneously into existence at that first meeting. The process of growth and change develops gradually. It takes time for the team to complete the journey from a collection of individuals to a cohesive, supportive, flexible and productive team. To do that they have to develop and change. It's a journey that takes them from the inhibited watchfulness of their first meetings, through conflict and the development of their own 'home-grown' set of rules and standards to, finally, become a team. That process needs help and support, which is what team building is about.

At this point, it's important to realize that the route that each team follows on this journey is unique to that team. It has to be, since that team itself is unique. But despite this uniqueness there are some basic factors that are common and important. One of these is about spending a lot of time together, even to the point of working in the same office or suite of offices. A lot of what happens in the team development process is informal. It's about getting to know each other, getting to know and respect each others' strengths and weaknesses, finding ways of working together. There often isn't time for this to take place outside the day-to-day operations of the project, it's a do-it-as-we-go process. It's also a process that takes place better and more quickly when people are in close proximity to each other. Walls and doors get in the way. In large teams this will mean dedicated space for the full-time staff. In small teams or teams with part-time members this means a dedicated 'team room' to which team members come to work on the team task and in which work-in-progress is left.

Another important element of building your team is the way in which conflict is handled.

Conflict is necessary to the process of becoming a real team. It occurs because people don't get on with each other, because people have different attitudes or sets of values and because people have different expectations. But most of all, in real teams, it occurs because all of the team are committed to doing their best for the team. Dealing with it isn't always easy; often feelings run high and voices are raised. But dealing with it is a must. If you sit on it, ignore it, push it under the surface of day-to day relations, then it'll just resurface elsewhere – and be the worse for it! If you're going to deal with it effectively then you may have to change the way that you think about it. It has to become a constructive opportunity rather than something to be endured.

The key factors in dealing with conflict are communication, communication and communication.

Frank, open talking and real listening are risky. But they are essential if you're going to have a real team. Taking the risk to be open in conflict can, on the down-side, lead to hurt feelings, hostility, enmity – even hatred. The up-side, though, is the hard-won mutual trust and interdependence that's essential to a real team.

Project teams

On the face of it, the task of creating a project team and then getting it to work doesn't appear to be a difficult one. After all, the sorts of people who are attracted to projects usually have that extra 'get up and go' that a project needs and one of the skills of good management is said to be that of 'recruiting good people and then letting them get on with it'.

But it isn't as simple as that – because project teams are different. Like the project itself, project teams are one-off. They are collections of people who come together for a defined and limited period of time. They do so in order to create a unique project outcome. These people may be part- or full-time members of the team and they will only be in that team for as long as their particular skills and knowledge are needed by the project. These factors generate a set of stresses that are particular to project teams. The result is that, in addition to the basic entry and team role criteria that were identified earlier in this chapter (see pages 82–4), we need project team members to have additional skills to cope with the stresses and strains of the project.

These are:

- Higher than average functional skills
- Sensitivity to the 'politics' of the project
- Strong problem-solving skills
- A willingness to share both successes and mistakes – and then move on to the next target.

The compositions of project teams often reflect the nature of the project outcome. For example, the team on a new office block project will contain civil engineers, structural engineers, electrical engineers and heating and ventilation specialists while the team for the production of a new book will involve a production editor, a graphic designer, a cost accountant, a printer, sales personnel and a marketing person. But if the people with these specialist skills are going to become a team then not only do they need to have the skills we identified earlier, they also need a project manager who is able to gain their trust and communicate with them. Inexperienced project managers often feel that in order to achieve this they need to know as much as the specialists in their team.

PROJECT TEAM CHECK OUT

Under each of the headings below ring a number which is nearest to the way that your project team operates – and then add up your total.

	Definitely applies to us	Applies to us	Not sure	Does not apply to us	Definitely doesn't apply to us
1 Process and size					
We come together easily and frequently	5	4	3	2	1
Our discussions are open and interactive	5	4	3	2	1
Everybody is involved in what goes on	5	4	3	2	1
We have enough people	5	4	3	2	1
2 Goal and targets					
We all know what we are trying to achieve	5	4	3	2	1
We all know how our performance will be measured	5	4	3	2	1
Our goals are realistic	5	4	3	2	1

Figure 6.2   Project team check out

	Definitely applies to us	Applies to us	Not sure	Does not apply to us	Definitely doesn't apply to us
3 Skills					
We have all the functional skills that we need	5	4	3	2	1
We spend time developing new skills	5	4	3	2	1
Our decisions involve us all	5	4	3	2	1
We use conflict constructively	5	4	3	2	1
4 Working approach					
The way we work draws on the skills and experience of all team members	5	4	3	2	1
We solve problems in fact-based ways	5	4	3	2	1
We can change the way we work	5	4	3	2	1

Key: Total

14–42   This seems to be more like a group than a team.

43–56   Good – check your scores with the rest of the team and use the results to focus your joint efforts to improve.

57–70   See if the rest of the team agree with your scores. If they do you are either a top-class team or all suffering from terminal group think.

But this is not so. Indeed, there is a saying amongst NASA project staff that a project manager who acts as if he is his own specialist staff would probably try to do open heart surgery on himself (or herself!) In other words, it isn't necessary or sensible for the project manager to be as good a specialist as they are. What is necessary and sensible is that the project manager can ask these specialists the 'right' questions and, more importantly, understand the answers.

Good project teams are rare animals. We often have project teams made up of people who are good at their job. They are good structural, clever piping engineers or excellent social workers, nurses or administrators – or even, for family projects, just good at being a member of a family. But we rarely have project teams of people who are good at their job *and* good at being a team member. Yet the value of a balanced and integrated project team cannot be understated. A project team like that – a project team that *works* – can overcome overwhelming difficulties, trials and tribulations and bring the project to a successful conclusion.

Use the questionnaire on pages 88–9 to check out your project team. and mistakes – and then move on to the next target.

Summary

Good teams make things happen. They work in ways that not only out-perform individual efforts but can also exceed those of the other sorts of social groups.

Teams are co-operative groups of people with shared objectives whose size rarely exceeds ten members. Members should be selected for their ability to work co-operatively with others and their ability to carry out the required team roles, as well as their functional skills.

Building a team starts with the generation of a joint team charter. It continues when the team spends time together and finds ways of handling conflict constructively. Project teams are special. They are collections of people who come together for a defined and limited period of time in order to create a unique project outcome. These people may be part- or full-time members of the team and they will only be in that team for as long as their particular skills and knowledge are needed by the project.

The members of successful project teams have higher than average functional skills, sensitivity to the 'politics' of both the project and its parent organization, strong problem-solving skills and a willingness to share both successes

7 MANAGING YOUR PROJECT MONEY

This chapter is about that most essential of project ingredients – money. By the end of it you'll have a clear idea of how your project's money needs can be estimated and budgeted. You'll also recognize the sort of factors that you need to take into account when you are generating that estimate and budget.

Money, money and money

In order to achieve our project's outcomes we must spend money. There are few, if any, exceptions to this rule. Indeed, money is so important to the project that its effective management is one of the must-have factors of successful project management. There are rules and procedures to help us in this management. These are usually grouped under the headings of Cost Accounting or Financial Project Management. We met some of these in Chapter 2 when we saw how financial ratios such as the project's 'rate of return', 'net present value' and 'profitability index' are used to help choose which project to implement.

However, the objective of this chapter is not to convert you into a cost accountant or even to make you over into a financial manager. It is to provide you with a basic understanding of the ways and means of your project money. This starts, in this chapter, by looking at the ways in which your project's money needs are estimated. It continues in Chapter 8 when we look at the ways that money is monitored and controlled. Once you have acquired that knowledge, it will make a substantial contribution to your ability to manage your project.

Cost, cost and more cost

Cost is the commonest word in the accountant's lexicon. But it rarely appears on its own and for that reason we need to look more closely at it and the ways in which it is used in our projects.

A cost, in the accounting sense, is something that springs into being when we spend money or anticipate that we will spend it. This happens when we buy our project materials – such as bricks or wood – or when we pay people for work that they have done on the project or when we rent machines to use on that project. The conventions of accounting tell us that these are called **material costs**, **labour costs** and **equipment costs** respectively. But costs can also be **direct**, as when we charge them directly to a specific project activity, or **indirect**, as when we allow them to be absorbed in the overall costs of the project. These indirect costs are also often called **overheads**.

But that's not the limit of the ways that we use to describe costs.

For our project costs can also be described as being **fixed**, as when they remain at the same level irrespective of the project workload, or **variable**, as when they vary with the rate of activity or project workload. The costs of our project also include the **standard** cost. This is a predetermined cost which is used, initially, to estimate the cost of a project activity and later, to monitor the cost performance of the project. It is generated from historic data and can be calculated for any activity or resource in the project. We can have, for example, a standard cost for laying bricks and a standard cost for the bricks themselves. Both would be in Rand or £ or $ per 1,000 bricks.

The predicted sum of these costs, i.e. the project's total cost estimate, is, as we saw in Chapter 1, one of those key features whose dimensions define the boundaries of the project. This predicted cost of a project can also exert a considerable influence upon whether that project is chosen – as we saw in Chapter 2. Later (in Chapter 8) we will see its role in the monitoring and controlling of the achieved or actual cost of a project.

What we need to do now is to look at how this predicted total cost is generated.

Hunches, guesstimates and estimates

Making sure that we have enough money to answer our project's needs isn't just important – it's *essential*.

But doing that is not one of those retrospective, after-the-spend, actions, nor is it a crystal ball based process designed to pluck arbitrary future figures out of the air. To answer our project's money needs we need to be able to predict accurately not only how much money is needed but also when it is needed.

The project estimate is the first step towards that knowledge.

This estimate is used in a number of ways. It can help us, for example, in the very early days of the project, to answer such questions as 'Is this new product worth further investigation?' or 'Is this book worth publishing?' It is also used in the process of deciding which of a number of competing projects represents the best investment for the funds of the organization or our personal money. Finally, once our project has been approved, this estimate becomes the core of the project's budget. That budget is used in the process of monitoring and controlling the project – in which actual spend is measured and then compared to the benchmark data of the estimate.

But the needs of these tasks are different. For example, to find out whether the idea of a project is worth further investigation we need an initial cost estimate with only a low level of accuracy. But when we come to decide if we want to release the money that the project needs, then we need a higher level of accuracy for our cost estimate. But, whatever their accuracy levels, it is important that these estimates are generated by the exercise of skill and judgement and using the best available data sources.

Doing that is not an exercise in risk taking or intuition. It is a logical exercise that is based on the best available information about:

■ the intended outcome of the project

■ the activities needed to achieve that outcome

■ the costs of those or similar activities.

But the level of detail and accuracy of the information available varies throughout the project's life cycle. In the Feasibility phase we have little detailed information. We may, for example, only have an approximate idea of the size, weight, output or floor area of our project's outcomes. This means that the estimate that we generate is based on a generalized 'broad brush' outcome definition, such as 'a four-seat family car' or 'a portable computer.' As such, it has a low level of accuracy. This sort of estimate is often used as a 'toe in the water' aimed at finding out whether it's worth exploring the project further. Its accuracy can be as low as ± 50%. The names given to this sort of estimate reflect this, such as a 'seat of the pants' estimate, or a 'ball-park' estimate or even an 'order of magnitude' estimate. Their use for any other purpose than very preliminary decision taking is not advised.

By the end of the Feasibility phase of the project's life cycle a go/no go decision will have been made about the project. To do this we need an estimate with a higher level of accuracy – usually ± 10%. To generate this we need more detail about our project outcome and the time-line of its generation. This detail is generated in two stages. These lead to what are called the Budget estimate and the Sanction estimate respectively. The first of these, the Budget estimate, has an accuracy level of ±20%. For projects with high cost levels or high levels of risk the Budget estimate is based on preliminary design work. In smaller, less complex or lower risk projects this design work is very limited and the Budget estimate might even be based on comparisons with other similar projects. This estimate, which is also called a Preliminary, Predesign or Feasibility estimate, is used to help us decide whether – or not – to start the detailed design of the project's outcome. This detailed design work is used to generate the second estimate – the Sanction estimate. With an accuracy level of ±10% the Sanction estimate is used to decide whether – or not – to proceed with the project. It also provides a foundation for the final estimate – the Definitive or Project Control estimate. This is only generated when the design work for the project outcome has been frozen – a step which, as we saw in Chapter 3 (page 42), enables us to create our project specification. It has an accuracy level of ± 5 to 10% and, as we will see later in Chapter 8, provides the benchmark for the monitoring and controlling of the project.

All of these estimates of the project's potential future cost are based on the information that is available.

Information, data, facts and figures

Given the importance of our project cost estimates it seems almost too obvious that we should use the best information that we can get to generate them. For most of us, however, the problem lies not in that information itself – but in where to find it.

When we generate our initial cost estimate we often only have a broad statement of intent about the project's outcome. This might tell us, for example, that the project is about creating a chemical plant to manufacture ammonia at the rate of 500 t/day, installing a drinks vending machine in an office block or taking a holiday in Hawaii. But, limited as this information is, it gets us started. For, by using the records of previous similar projects, indicative costs quoted by manufacturers or a friend's memory of the cost of his or her holiday, we can generate a 'ball-park' or an 'order of magnitude' estimate of the project's likely cost.

But if we are to increase the accuracy of our estimate then we need more information – information about the activities to be undertaken and resources needed to support those activities and, most importantly, their anticipated costs. The first of these, the activity information, is important. For without it we may find that the cost estimate for our project for the installation of a drinks vending machine doesn't include the cost of providing drainage of waste water and spillages away from the machine or even the cost of providing sufficient electrical power for the machine's safe operation. One way of avoiding this sort of situation is to sit down and generate a list. This should cover, firstly, the areas in which work is needed and secondly, the actual work that is needed. An example of the first sort of list – which is often called a Work Breakdown Schedule (WBS) – is given in Figure 7.1.

VENDING MACHINE PROJECT
WORK BREAKDOWN SCHEDULE

Phase 1: Activity areas

Supply machine
Selection of location
Provision of electrical power
Provision of potable water
Provision of waste water drainage
Provision of storage for consumables
Provision of solid waste facilities – cups etc.

Figure 7.1   Example of Phase 1 of a Work Breakdown Schedule

On a small project – such as our vending machine project – this may be all that you need to do. Once you have decided which machine to buy and where the machine and its storage facilities are to be located then you can use this list as a check-list when you get contractors to provide quotations for each or all the other separate activities.

On a large project, life is more complicated and your WBS will need to have several levels – each with ascending degrees of detail – for each of the types of estimate that we identified earlier in this chapter. This process goes on until you reach the final and definitive version of this WBS – that contained in the project specification.

The data that we use to generate the costs contained in each of these levels of estimate comes from a variety of sources. These can include:

- web sites
- previous projects
- suppliers
- contractors
- cost engineering consultants
- trade and government cost indices
- trade magazines
- professional journals and publications
- reference and textbooks.

However, you must remember that, however good these sources are, in the end the accuracy of your estimate lies in your hands. If you miss something important out or add something unnecessary in, then it could make the difference between the success or failure of your project.

Top-down or bottom-up

The methods that we use to generate estimates will change with the level of accuracy required.

In the early part of the project life cycle – when levels of accuracy as low as ± 50% are acceptable – 'top-down' methods can be used. These, as we will soon see, start from either the size of the project outcome or from the cost of a major part of that outcome. In the later stages – when levels of accuracy as high as ± 5–10% are needed – 'bottom-up' methods are used. These are much more detailed and often start from the detail of individual work items.

Top-down

Top-down estimating methods start from information that contains the lowest level of detail about the project. This can be either a statement about the size of the project – as in a 200,000 m^2 warehouse, a 200-page book, 100 t/day ammonia plant or a 14-day holiday in Hawaii – or the size and cost of its most significant item.

When we use the size of the project outcome to generate our cost estimate we use a method that is called the exponential method. The cost estimate for the new project is generated by multiplying the known cost of a completed similar project by the ratio of the size of new outcome to the size of the completed project's outcome raised to a given power – or exponent. When you express this as an equation it looks like this:

Cost of new project $= $ Cost of old project $\times$ (S_{new}/S_{old}) $^{0.66}$
where S_{new} $=$ size or capacity of your new project
S_{old} $=$ size or capacity of old project.

Complicated? – no, not really, as you'll see from the following example:

Let's say that we want to estimate the cost of building a warehouse with a floor area of 200,000 m^2. An identical warehouse with a floor area of 150,000 m^2, completed last month, had a total material and erection cost of, say, £250,000. We can estimate that the cost of the new, larger, warehouse will be:

£250,000 $\times$ (200,000/150,000) $^{0.66}$
or £302,273.

If we had ratioed these costs in direct proportion to the size of the warehouses we would have estimated the cost as:

£250,000 $\times$ (200,000/150,000)
or £333,333 – which is over 10% more!

The exponents used depend, to some extent, on the nature of your project. In most situations an exponent in the range of 0.6 to 0.75 is acceptable but there is some evidence that software projects require an exponent which is as high as 1.20. When you are using this method you need to:

■ take care to ensure that you are comparing like with like

■ remember that the accuracy of the result is as low as ±50%.

The second of the top-down methods that we can use is called the factorial or parametric estimating method. This method of cost estimation starts from a detailed and accurate cost for a core item in the project outcome – such as a boiler in a boiler house project, a vending machine in a drinks vending machine project or the hotel costs for a 14-day holiday in Hawaii.

This core cost is then used to find the cost of the other bits of the project – such as piping, electrical services, airline flights, etc. For example, if we know that the cost of the vending machine is £2,000 then, by the use of factors, we can estimate that the cost of the water supply might be (£2,000 × 0.12) = £240 and the cost of the electrical services might be (£2,000 × 0.08) = £160. When we add together all of these costs, we arrive at the cost estimate for the project. There are a number of sources of the factors and when you are using this method you need to be sure that:

■ the factors are developed from a data base that is relevant, accurate and large enough

■ the project outcome is scalable.

Bottom-up

Bottom-up methods of estimating start from the information contained in the project's Work Breakdown Schedule (WBS). The greater the detail in this schedule, the higher the level of accuracy of the estimate. As we saw earlier the highest level of WBS detail exists in its final and definitive version contained in the project specification. The most accurate bottom-up estimates use this level of the WBS to estimate the cost of individual work items. These are then accumulated into the total cost of the project. On most projects this involves a lot of work – and work costs money – so the project manager will need to weigh the cost of generating such an estimate against the value of its accuracy.

Whatever the level of accuracy we chose, the information about the individual work items that we use has to be both realistic and well founded. For example, none of our project work starts with instantly high levels of activity. Like all human activities their work rates start low, rise, stabilize and then fall, to cease at the completion of the work item. These differing work rates will obviously influence either the labour that we need for the task or, if that is limited, the time taken to complete the task.

We'll look at this in more detail. Let's assume that we need a total of 600 person hours to paint the interior of a new office block and that the project schedule says that this has to be completed in three 40-hour working weeks. If we divide the people hours by the hours available, i.e. (600/40 × 3), this tells us that we need 5 people. But this apparently logical calculation ignores the fact that work rates start low, rise, and then fall. One way of allowing for these varying rates is to assume that the initial low, but rising, work-rate phase lasts for a fifth of the total calendar time available, i.e. 24 hours or three 8-hour days, and that the run-down phase at the end lasts for 30% of that total calendar time, i.e. 36 hours or four and a half 8-hour working days. The peak activity level will take place over the seven and a half 8-hour days between these phases. If we average the rate at which work takes place during both the initial and final phases of the task then we can calculate that:

$$\text{Number of people} = \frac{600 \text{ people hours}}{(3 + 4.5) \text{ days at 4 hours per day}}$$
equivalent + 7.5 days at 8 hours per day

or Number of people = 600/90 = 6.66 people.

Remember that if we had assumed a constant activity rate throughout the whole of this 15-day period then our estimate of the number of people required would have been 5 – which is a third too low!

Below and above the line

We have already seen that the costs that make up our estimates can be described in various ways.

These include labour and material costs that can be direct or indirect depending on whether they are directly charged to a particular project activity or to the overall business of running the project. An example of an indirect labour cost would be the salary costs of the project manager, secretaries, clerks etc. An example of a direct material cost would be the bricks, concrete, sand, wood, glass, tiles, etc. that are used in an office block project.

But we also may need equipment to complete the tasks that are demanded by our project. This equipment can be the scaffolding that we need to access the roof of our office block, the computers that we use to schedule and monitor our project or the suitcases that we need for our holiday in Hawaii. This equipment can be hired, leased or bought. But, however they are acquired, the cost of doing so needs to be included in your project cost estimate. All of these are called, in accounting terms, 'above-the-line' costs.

There is another, just as important, group of costs that are called 'below-the-line' costs. Amongst these are the costs that accountants usually group under the collective title of 'miscellaneous fees'. These indirect or overhead costs can include design charges from outside agencies, consultancy fees, inspection fees, the costs of insuring against claims for loss and damage from other people, tax liability and our holiday insurance against illness, cancellation etc.

These 'below-the-line' costs also include an inflation allowance. You will remember, from Chapter 2, that the Net Present Value method of assessing a project proposal took account of the fact that the value of our money changes with time. If the life span of our project exceeds six months then we need to protect ourselves against the effects of this change. We do this by including an inflation allowance in our cost estimate – as a below-the-line cost. The inflation rate used to calculate this allowance comes from government and industry predictions. On very extended projects, this inflation can be covered by a cost review clause that allows for the sanctioning of additional funds if inflation indices exceed a defined level.

Generating an estimate is a complicated task and one that, by its nature, attempts to anticipate the future costs of events. Obviously, there are risks in doing so and a project manager can find himself or herself hostage to tomorrow's fortunes. This can come about for a number of reasons. Mistakes are made, information and costs are left out of the estimate, currency exchange rates change, new technology becomes available or earthquakes, hurricanes or strikes happen. What our estimate needs is a below-the-line sum that covers for these eventualities. This is called a contingency allowance.

The contingency allowance has a typical value of around 5% of the total project estimate. But it is not intended to cover for changes in project scope or for failures in the estimating process. It is intended to act as a hedge against unknown or difficult-to-predict events. Its value for your project will be influenced by things like the risk level or novelty of the project (see Chapter 2) and an assessment of the real likelihood of events such as earthquakes, hurricanes or strikes.

Budgets

The point at which our estimate changes into our budget is a significant one for the project. It is one of those project milestones, one of those significant points that mark a major change in the pace or rhythm of the project.

It usually occurs around the point at which the project's money is sanctioned. The shift from being an estimate to becoming a budget results in two significant changes in the information that is so vital to the financial well-being of our budget.

The first of these lies in the fact that the budget tells us not only *what* is to be spent – as the estimate did – it also tells us *when* that expenditure is to take place. The estimate that we have brought together now becomes a time-based statement of our financial intent, one in which the sequence of our expenditure from the beginning to the end of the project is defined. To do this the budget draws heavily on the content of the project plan. As we saw in Chapter 4, this tells us about the starts, finishes and resource demands of our project's activities. The relationship between project plan and project budget is a close one (see Figure 7.2). So close that it provides us with one of the mechanisms by which we can 'fine-tune' our management of the project.

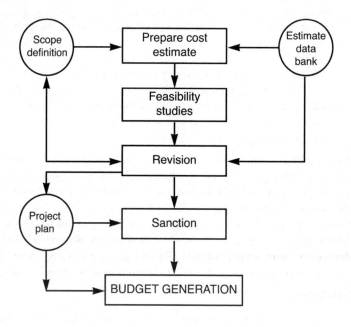

Figure 7.2   Budgets, plans and estimates

The second of these changes is just as important. For with that shift – from estimate to budget – and the sanction process that accompanies it, this financial information changes from being an expression of our intent, a forecast or a prediction, to becoming a limit of what we can spend in our project. This is a significant change. It means that our project budget not only tells us *when* our expenditure is to take place, it now also tells us what the *limit* or *boundary* of that expenditure is to be. Our project's budget provides a baseline, a datum level, against which we can measure, monitor and control our project expenditure. This is what we look at in the next chapter.

Summary

The creation of accurate estimates is vital to the success of a project. But generating an estimate is not an exercise in risk taking or intuition – it is a logical exercise that is based on the available information about the intended outcome of the project, the activities needed to achieve that outcome and the information that we have about the costs of identical or even similar activities.

The types of estimate that we generate are:

- 'ball-park', 'seat of the pants', 'order of magnitude' estimate (± 50%)
- budget, predesign, feasibility estimate (±20%)
- sanction estimate (± 10%)
- definitive estimate (± 5–10%)

These estimates can be top-down – using exponential or factorial estimating techniques – or bottom-up – using costs generated from Work Breakdown Schedule (WBS) data by use of labour, material and equipment costs. Both of these will require additional 'below-the-line' costs such as insurance and tax charges and allowances for inflation and contingencies. When a project is sanctioned its estimate becomes its budget – a source of information about what is to be spent and when it is to be spent. This budget will enable our project spend to be both monitored and controlled.

8 | MONITORING AND CONTROLLING YOUR PROJECT

This chapter looks at the ways in which a project is monitored and controlled and the contributions that these can make to its success. By the end of it you should have a better understanding of the ways and means by which the project's progress is measured, monitored, compared to its goals and targets and kept on course.

Full steam ahead

Once your project is underway, the pace of its activity increases rapidly. Statements of future intent become matters of everyday reality. The brave prospects of forward-looking plans become history. With all this change and progress there also comes, inevitably, the erosive drift of time. Risks that we had thought remote become real and distinct possibilities, evolving into present certainties.

The nature of these difficulties can be as various as the flowers in spring. For example, important material deliveries can be delayed, vital equipment breaks down, key personnel can go sick or be re-assigned to other projects or new technology fails to deliver. It can snow, rain or hail in summer, Head Office can put a freeze on all project spending and our children can catch measles on the eve of our holiday departure.

But not all of our difficulties are as major or as serious as these. More often, the problems of our projects consist of a multitude of apparently minor, trivial incidents; incidents whose effects, though small, can nevertheless accumulate to significant levels and then cause delays, cost overruns and shortfalls in outcome performance or quality. The reasons for and causes of these deviations from our plan are also various. They can come about because we fail to plan with adequate foresight or because we ignore or discount real risks or, most human of all, because we make mistakes.

In short, things don't always happen the way that we planned that they would.

This sort of situation crops up on almost every project. Very, very few projects are exempt and coping with it is one of the key skills shown by experienced project managers. But when these drifts and deviations occur, what is important is not that they happen – since they are largely history by the time we become aware of them – but the ways that we respond to them. For if that response is to be effective; if it is to protect and maintain our ability to create the outcomes of our project at the scheduled time with the desired performance at the right cost and quality, then it must contain two vital elements.

The first of these is contained in the ways in which we react to these differences between what we planned and what we have been able to achieve. These are, in effect, the tools that we use to solve our projects' problems. These we will look at in the next chapter (Chapter 9).

The second of these vital elements is discussed in this chapter. It is about the ways and means that we use, firstly, to tell us when the activities of our project are not as they ought to be and, secondly, to correct or limit the effects of those deviations from our project plan. In short, this chapter is about the ways in which we monitor and control our projects.

Monitoring

When we monitor something, we observe, measure or test it.

Let's assume, for example, that we want to monitor the hours of sunshine in Tucson, Arizona, or the amount of rain that falls in Liverpool, England. The first thing that we need to do is to find a way of measuring this sunshine or rainfall. But not just any old way will do; it needs to be a way that is reliable, accurate, economic and repeatable. Once we have found this then we can start to measure the sunshine or rainfall – probably on a daily basis. The daily data that we generate needs to be recorded. Those records need to be organized so that we can, for instance, compare month with month or year with year. We might also want to analyze this data in ways that tell us about long-term trends, patterns or other effects. Other people might be interested in the results of all this activity. Because of this, the ways in which we record and express these records of sunshine or rainfall need to be both accessible and understandable.

The ways in which we monitor the progress of our projects are similar. But instead of providing us with passive numbers, our project monitoring provides us with active information. The answers to such questions as 'Is this activity on schedule?', 'Have we overspent the project budget?' or 'What is the project's probable finish date?' are important. They tell us if our project is – or isn't – on plan. But that's not all that our project monitoring tells us. We need to know about the where and when of our project's drifts and deviations. For, unlike our monitoring of Tucson's sunshine or Liverpool's rainfall, the results of this monitoring lead us on to another vital element in the management of our project – that of controlling it. Once we have the answers to our questions then we can begin to do something about the cause of these differences – and thus bring the project back 'on course'.

Project monitoring – what and when

The effective monitoring of our project is important. It tells us where we are. From that we can predict where we are likely to be in the future and then we can work out what we need to do to influence or change that future. It also provides us with the sort of performance measurement that we can use to motivate our project team.

But this monitoring cannot be an indiscriminate across-the-board activity. That would give us too much data and too little time to analyze or react to it. Our project monitoring needs to be focused so that its contribution to our projects is not only relevant, it's also timely and maximized.

The first step that we take towards that goal is to decide:

■ what we are going to monitor, and

■ how often we are going to monitor it.

The choice of *what* we monitor is one that must be made with care. For if we monitor too few or too unimportant things then we might miss the drift or movement of a key aspect and not be able to react until it is too late. If we monitor too many things, then we finish up with too much data and too little time to analyze it. What we monitor must also be related to the key features of our project – Cost, Performance and Time. The closer that relationship is, the better the result. But that's not all that we must consider. For if what we monitor is going to help us manage our project then not only must it be related to those key features, it must also be, in itself, significant, believable and easy to measure and understand.

Finding project 'pulse-points' that meet these criteria isn't always easy – but it can be done. For example, on a project to write a new book we can monitor the number of words written, and on a project to redecorate a room we can monitor the wall area repainted or re-papered. Don't forget that you can also monitor how things are going by that well-known technique of 'management-by-walking-about'. There's no real substitute for getting out there, actually seeing what is happening and talking to the people involved. A decision 'on the ground' can be the proverbial 'stitch in time that saves nine'.

Of course, even these 'pulse-point' measurements don't tell us the whole story. To gain that, we need to be able to link them back to those two core sources of project information – the project plan and the project budget. Both of these provide us with information that will help us to decide the other key aspect of our monitoring – when or how often we do it.

Deciding the 'right' frequency of our monitoring measurements is as important as deciding what to monitor. Too often and we drown in data, too seldom and we miss the early drift that leads to later major deviations.

THE PROJECT ORGANIZATION FRAMEWORK

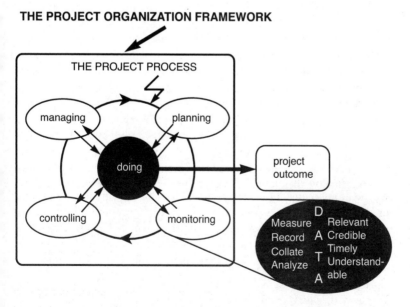

Figure 8.1   Monitoring and the project process

Getting it right depends on things like the overall length of the project and its risk level. For example, on most long projects, measurement and reporting on a weekly frequency would be sufficient. On short projects – in which the events of a single day can be crucial – measurement and reporting on a daily or even half daily frequency would be warranted. High-risk projects demand, for obvious reasons, more frequent measurements than low-risk projects. Whatever you decide is right for you, remember that in this – as in other areas – regularity is important. Regular monitoring keeps us in touch with our project and that enables us to manage it successfully.

The project plan and monitoring

When we first create our project plan it is about our intended future actions. At that time its value lies in the ways that it helps us to estimate both the cost and duration of the project. Once our project gets underway that changes. For then our plan becomes a road map for our journey, a 'this-is-what-you-do-next' guide for our actions.

But that isn't all that it does for us. For we can also use that plan to monitor the progress of our project. When we do this the plan will tell us whether its activities are up to, or behind, schedule. If we find that they are behind schedule then we need to decide what we are going to do about that. The project plan can act as a framework within which we evaluate the options for decisions that we must then make. We can use it as a base-line from which we can develop hybrid or alternative plans. This will help us to see the results of our 'what if we...?' proposals and test the feasibility of our options. To do this our plans must be, as we saw in Chapter 4 clear, unambiguous, easily understood and, above all, capable of change. Changing our project plan is also one of the ways in which we control our project, as we shall see later in this chapter. But if that change is to be effective then it must always be preceded by and based on the data generated by the process of monitoring.

We also saw in Chapter 4 that most information is best presented in a graphic visual form. The use of the project plan for monitoring is no exception to this. The filled-in bars of the Gantt chart tell us about the progress of our activities. Numbers also have their place and we can represent our progress and compare it to our targets by the data recorded on the nodes and arrows of the AOA networks or the nodes of our Precedence networks.

Milestones

One of the most common ways of monitoring the progress of our project uses milestones.

These, like the milestones of our highways, can be used to mark the stages of our project's journey from start to completion. They are best set at the end or beginning of an activity – for ease of identification – and are usually limited to Critical Path activities. On a Gantt chart they can be indicated graphically by an icon such as a diamond (◊). The unfilled ◊ represents a scheduled milestone and the filled ♦, a completed milestone. Our progress towards their achievement can also be reported in the words and dates of a milestone report that contains such information as shown in Figure 8.2.

Milestone no.	Scheduled date	Anticipated date	Achieved date	Notes
4	25th Oct.	–	24th Oct.	Completed ahead of schedule
5	13th Dec.	15th Dec.	–	Material delivery delay anticipated

Figure 8.2   Milestones report example

The milestones of our projects tell us, as on our highways and roads, how far we have travelled. But they are not the only tool that we can use to monitor the status of our projects.

Limits

We can also find out how our projects are progressing by using Limit Testing.

This involves comparing the current value of say, project milestone achievement, to the value that we had planned. If there is a difference, then we need to know more about it. The larger the difference is, the quicker we need to know about it and the more detail we require. This technique can also, with a little imagination, be applied to other critical aspects of the project such as activity rates or project spend. Its advantages include its compatibility with most project management information systems (PMIS) and the ease of its operation.

The responses and actions that are triggered by a difference – between planned and achieved – need to be relevant to its size. For example, a milestone achievement rate that is 5% low will initiate an investigation, whereas a 10% underachievement would cause tighter control procedures to be initiated and higher frequencies of reporting.

ABC analysis

Another technique that we can use to monitor our project is Pareto or ABC analysis.

Commonly used in inventory management, ABC analysis is based on the work of Vilfredo Pareto, a 19th-century Italian economist. Pareto identified the empirical relationship that is often called the 80–20 rule. When used to control inventories this identifies the 20% of stocks that are responsible for 80% of total inventory costs. These are called Class A items. In our project we can use this rule to identify the 20% of activities that are responsible for 80% of project labour costs or the 20% of materials that are responsible for 80% of the project's material costs. Once we know which these Class A activities or materials are then we can adjust our measurement and reporting routines to make sure that they are measured and monitored more frequently. We can also extend our use of the 80–20 rule so that it takes into account more than just cost. For, having identified the A class items or activities of our spend we can then reclassify these in terms of their use on the project's critical path activities – and then readjust our monitoring and reporting accordingly. This way we monitor for those items and activities that are important in relation to two of our project's dimensions – Cost and Time.

It's also worth noting that both ABC analysis and Limit Testing can make major contributions to the management of another of the project's scarce resources – the project manager's time – since he or she is only involved when the pre-set limit has been exceeded or when critical items are delayed or overspent.

The project budget and monitoring

In Chapter 7 we saw that the budget tells us not only *what* is to be spent but also *when* that spend is to take place. This sequence of project expenditure is defined from the beginning to the end of the project.

This flow of cash must be monitored. If we fail to do that then we put at risk our ability to achieve the targets that we have set for our project; targets that are defined in terms of Cost, Time and Performance. We have already seen how Limit Testing and ABC analysis can help us with this monitoring. Another of the ways that we can use is what is often called the S curve, as illustrated in Figure 8.3.

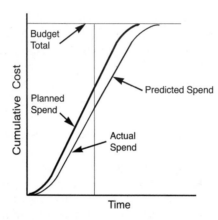

Figure 8.3   The S curve

What the S curve shows us are the trends in and differences between the project's budgeted, actual and predicted spend. But what it doesn't show us is the causes of the differences between the planned and actual spend – and these are important, as we shall soon see.

Let's assume that, as in the S curve shown above, the cumulative actual cost of our project is less than what we had planned – an apparently comfortable situation, you might think. But this could have occurred because either the work completed was on schedule but cost less than we had planned or because the work completed was behind schedule but had cost more than we had planned.

The differences between these two explanations are important – not least to the ways in which we manage the future actions of our project. For if our future costs are likely to be less than the budgeted level, then we can use that difference. It can be used, for example, to either invest in additional resources – and thus complete the project earlier than planned – or to enhance the performance of the project by providing additional features. On the other hand, if our future costs look likely to exceed that budgeted level, then we need to make sure not only that we find out why that has happened but also that we control that cost over-run.

Earned value

One of the ways in which we can solve this riddle – and find out what is actually happening – is to use the technique called Earned Value Analysis (EVA). This is used on many projects and has been refined and modified by the US Department of Defence into the Cost/Schedule Control System (C/SCS) for projects. C/SCS and EVA both attempt to show us what are the relationships between variances in cost and schedule and project performance.

Here's a simple example. Let's assume that we need to build a brick wall. As this is a large wall, we allow a period of fifteen hours for its completion – including the time needed for the hand excavation and preparation of its foundation. The total budgeted labour cost is \$80. But after 15 hours our monitoring tells us that all was not going well. There had been problems with the foundations. We find that \$85 of direct labour costs has been billed and the job isn't complete. Only three-quarters of the bricks have been laid!

So, what can we find out from this and – more importantly – what can we do about it?

Earned Value Analysis (EVA) tells us that after 15 hours:

- **Budgeted Cost of Work Performed (BCWP)** – or **Earned Value** is equal to:

   (Units of work actually done $\times$ budgeted unit cost)

   $= \$(0.75 \times 80)$ or $\$(0.75 \times 15 \times 80/15) = \$60.0$

- **Actual Cost of Work Performed (ACWP)** is equal to:

   (Units of work actually done $\times$ actual unit cost)

   $= \$85$

■ **Budgeted Cost of the Work Scheduled (BCWS)** – or **Planned Value** is equal to:

(Units of work scheduled × budgeted unit cost)
= $80

From these three figures we can work out:

Cost Variance (CV)

This is the algebraic difference between the **Earned Value** and the **Actual Cost** – or (**BCWP – ACWP**) – and is equal to:

($60 – $85) = a negative variance of $25 or 42% of the Earned Value.

A positive value for this variance represents a favourable position and a negative value, an unfavourable one.

Schedule Variance (SV)

This is the algebraic difference between the **Earned Value** of the work performed and the **Budgeted Value of the Work Planned** – or (**BCWP – BCWS**) – and is equal to:

($60 – $80) = a negative variance of $20 or 33% of the Earned Value.

A positive value for this variance represents a favourable position and a negative value, an unfavourable one.

These variances not only tell the project manager about the true, rather than the apparent, state of the project, they also give him or her pointers as to where actions will help to bring the costs of the project back under control. In this case, the larger Cost Variance and the fact that we know that there had been problems with digging the foundations tell us that we need to look at machine – rather than hand – excavation of foundations.

A simpler and easy-to-use variant of EV Analysis is the Critical Ratio. This ratio is made up of (Actual Progress/Scheduled Progress) × (Budgeted Cost/Actual Cost) and its value tells us whether we need to investigate further. For example, the value of the Critical Ratio for our wall would have been:

(0.75) × ($80/$85) = 0.705

When the value of this ratio falls below 1.0 this tells us that there is a need to investigate a below-par performance. A value of 1.0 indicates that all is well with our project and a value above 1.0 indicates a need to investigate an above par performance. The further the ratio is away from 1.0, the more urgent the need to investigate.

Monitoring – reports and meetings

We have already seen that effective communication is vital to the success of the project.

Once our project is underway, most of this communication is about the what, how and why of the project's progress. One of the ways that we can keep people informed is by progress reports. These need to be issued regularly, though they can also be issued when a special event or problem warrants it. While their primary purpose is to report the general progress of the project to the client – the project's paymaster – they should also be available to other stakeholders. These reports are an important element in the communication patterns of the project. As such they have to be understandable, concise and based on facts. They are generally read by busy people, so brevity is also desirable. Supporting data, where required, should be nested in appendices. Routine progress reports – in the form of tables of figures, Gantt charts or AOA networks – should be presented with limited comment. These reports are often complementary to another method of reporting project progress – the project meeting.

Project meetings are important. They are the major arena within which project stakeholders exert their influence. As such they possess a considerable potential for conflict and disagreement. Because of this our project meetings must be conducted in ways that are clearly and effectively focused on the achievement of results and targets. Managing a project meeting that achieves these objectives represents a real skill on the part of the project manager.

But even this skill must have a backcloth against which it is acted out. For our project meeting this consists of: agendas – that state the business to be discussed; minutes – that briefly record what was decided and who is to do what; and briefing papers, such as project progress reports – that ensure the participants are well informed. These project meetings should be brief – no longer than one and a half hours – events from which participants emerge better informed about the project, having been involved in decisions on key project issues and with a better understanding of their own role in the project.

We've already noted that the exchange of factual information plays an important role in these meetings. It's a role that is further enhanced when participants feel able to exchange opinions, views and feelings about those facts. Achieving this means limiting the size of the project meeting – probably to a maximum of ten people – and chairing the meeting with skill and sensitivity. Indeed, the effectiveness with which the chairperson role is carried out can make or break the project meeting.

Effective chairpeople are concerned with the process of the meeting, rather than advocating or representing a particular viewpoint, line or policy. Chairing a project meeting in this way is often not easy for project managers, who are, after all, responsible for the successful completion of the project. But project managers rarely act in teams of one. Delegating the responsibility for presentation of a particular viewpoint to another member of the project team is often an effective way of presenting material – without compromising the project manager's impartiality. In the end, a project meeting is only as good as the people who attend. If the meeting is to be valuable and effective, then these people must be willing to engage in a constructive dialogue with each other. Given that, and an experienced and capable chairperson, the meetings of our project not only help the ways in which we monitor our projects, they also help us to keep the project on course – by controlling it.

Controlling

When we find that the activities of our project are not as they ought to be, then we need to do something about it.

These detours from our project plan and budget can be about any aspect of the three features or dimensions of our project – Time, Cost and Performance. The ways and means that we use to correct or limit their effects – to regulate them – can be just as various. We may need, for example, to recruit additional contract labour to correct schedule slippage or to reduce staffing levels to bring activities with potential early completion dates back in line. Unexpected technical problems may need to be solved by additional and unbudgeted R&D spend, or market fluctuations may bring an unexpected bonus of lower than estimated raw material prices.

But the actions that we take must have a single exclusive objective – to bring our project back in line with its plan or its budget. That is, these actions, by which we control our project, must act to reduce the difference between what is actually happening and our project plan or budget.

We've already seen that we can use the project plan to help us choose what these actions are to be. It can help us identify the probable results of our 'what if we...?' proposals and test the feasibility of our options. In Chapter 2 we looked at some of the ways that help us to choose between one proposed project and another. These can also be used to help us choose between one possible action and another. The next chapter, Chapter 9, tells us about some of the ways that we can use to identify effective and economic solutions to the problems that can cause a project to drift 'off-course'. But, whatever we decide to do and however we arrive at that decision, our control of our project must have its roots in our monitoring. This lets us know when the activities of our project aren't as they ought to be. Then, and only then – when we have that information – are we able to act to correct or limit the effects of those variations from our project plan.

But these actions, if they are to be successful, must be distinctive in their style and nature. They need, for example, to be appropriate – to the project, its outcome and its stakeholders. They also need to be quick-acting – to ensure that the variation doesn't get out of control, and cost effective – to ensure that the cost of our control doesn't exceed its value. But most of all, the actions by which we control our project need to be compatible with the variation's size and polarity. This means that there is no place in our project for sledgehammers to crack nuts or cups of water

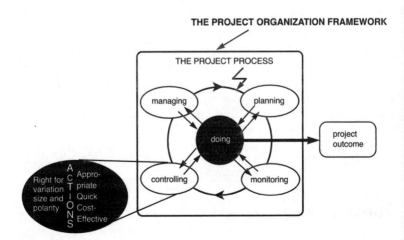

Figure 8.4   Controlling and the project process

to douse infernos. The size or power of the actions that we take to control our projects must be appropriate to the size of the monitored departure from our plan or budget.

Getting this right can sometimes take real skill and judgement. There's never enough data to enable us to be absolutely sure. Our actions must be prompt and quick if they are to be effective. Whatever we do, we must also be sure that our actions generate results that oppose the forces that are driving our project 'off-course'. This means that while it's right to reduce expenditure in the face of a cost over-run, we also need to find out what the real cause of that over-run is. As we saw earlier in this chapter, Earned Value Analysis (EVA) can help here, as can some of the techniques we'll look at in Chapter 9.

But some of the differences identified by our monitoring will have causes that are too significant for the day-by-day remedial actions of our project control. These can range from the substantial, as when new technology becomes available, to the small, as when detailed design work progresses and shows us a better way to do something. Some of these will offer us the chance to do things in ways that are better than the ways we had planned. Others will have their roots in our mistakes and errors. Whatever their origin, nature or size might be, all of these significant changes have the potential to drive our project 'off-course' in terms of either its duration, cost or the nature and quality of its outcome. It is essential that we use our project change control procedure to control these modifications to our project. This, as we saw in Chapter 3, enables us to identify any changes from the project's 'base' line – as contained in the project specification – and then to evaluate, approve or reject those proposed changes at the earliest possible opportunity. Effective change procedures are an important tool in the way that we control our project.

Above all, the control that the project manager exerts must be:

- based on facts, rather than on opinions
- targeted solely towards keeping the project in line with its planned duration, cost and outcome.

Summary

Things don't always happen the way that we planned. Monitoring and controlling are aimed at counteracting the effects of these differences, and putting our project back 'on-line'.

Project monitoring involves the actions of measuring, recording, collating and analyzing data which is relevant, credible, timely and understandable. It is connected to the project plan and the project budget and can use project milestones, limit testing, the 80–20 rule, S curves, Earned Value Analysis and Critical Ratios. This 'state-of-the-project' information is passed to project stakeholders by the use of project progress reports and project meetings.

Project control is aimed at reducing the gap between what is actually happening and what we had planned should happen. It is rooted in our project monitoring and its actions should be appropriate, quick and cost effective, and should reflect the size and polarity of the differences between actuality and our plan. Getting these actions right can take real skill and judgement – because there's never enough data or time. Whatever we do must be based on facts – rather than on opinions – and be targeted solely towards keeping the project in line with its planned duration, cost and outcome.

9 | **SOLVING YOUR PROJECT PROBLEMS**

This chapter looks at our project problems and reviews some of the ways that we can find solutions for them. By the end of it you should have a better understanding of some of the techniques that we can use to recognize and understand project problems and, most importantly, to identify their potential solutions.

Problems, problems and problems

In the last chapter we saw that monitoring tells us about our project's 'state of health'. Some days what it tells us is good: our project is 'on schedule', its critical ratio is close to 1.0 and its Cost and Schedule Variances are low. On other days, however, we are told that things are not as we desired or planned. When this happens we usually say that we have a 'problem'.

Problems and projects seem to go together like strawberries and cream or sausage and mash. Problems crop up, on almost a daily basis, in every project. These can be large or small and their consequences can be significant or trifling. But size and consequence aren't their only characteristics. For some of them come fully equipped with structure, certainty and a range of clear alternatives for their solution whereas others appear diffuse, uncertain, lacking structure and without solutions. In the folklore of project management most of our project problems are said to be caused by people and to have roots that reach back into the early days of the project.

But whatever their source, focus or nature might be, they contain the seeds of potential disruption for our project. For they all have the ability to cause delays or generate cost overruns or to lead to shortfalls in outcome performance or quality.

There can be little doubt that problem-solving is a key ability for the effective project manager. It is one of those 'must-have' skills whose presence makes a major contribution to project success and whose absence can only lead to failure. As a would-be effective project manager, you can either become a problem-solver – or you can become a part of your project's problems.

A perfect world

In a perfect world, our project problems would arrive from our monitoring, neatly packaged and wrapped. They would contain all the data that we needed to define and understand them. Their arrival would be timely, giving us plenty of time to identify their best solution. We might even recognize them as problems that we had met – and solved – before.

Our approach to these paragons of problems would be logical and linear. First, we would review their symptoms. This would help us to identify or confirm their exact nature. Then we would generate a range of possible solutions – each complete with relevant data. Finally, we would carefully choose and implement one of these.

But occasionally, in this perfect world, we might come across a problem that presented itself in ways that were far from being ideal. It would have limited data, no structure and no clear alternatives. Its arrival would be tardy and overdue leaving us little time to do anything other than to react to it.

In the real world – rather than this perfect one – most, if not all, of our project problems are like this. We rarely have enough information or enough time to be sure that we can identify, with absolute certainty, their nature. As a consequence we can seldom be sure that the solution that we choose is the best one. On some projects – such as development projects or high risk, very innovative projects – this sort of uncertainty is endemic.

But should we be surprised about all this? After all, our projects have, as we saw in Chapter 1, outcomes that are unique and it would be surprising if their problems didn't share that characteristic. Despite, or perhaps because of, this uncertainty, the first step towards solving our problems lies in defining them.

Frequency and consequence

But how much definition do we need? Do we need to know all the facts, details, implications and subtleties of a problem before we can solve it, or can we cope with less than a complete picture?

Part of the answer to this question lies with:

- how often the problem occurs, and
- what are the problem's potential consequences.

For example, we need to know more about a recurring problem – because it keeps happening and, perhaps, because our previous attempts to solve it have failed. Infrequent or occasional problems appear to be less demanding in their data needs.

This can and does change when we look at the consequences of the problem. What we then begin to see is that infrequent problems with unacceptable – because of their cost or nature – consequences would demand and receive more attention; whereas low frequency problems with limited or acceptable consequence receive little attention. We saw this in Chapter 2 when we looked at whether we should reduce the risks associated with our possible future projects. For our problems, this marriage of frequency and the consequence is just as important. For it will give us – even if we have to estimate or guess both the consequence and the frequency – a basis on which to prioritize our response to a problem. If either of these are high then we need further data to define and solve the problem. If either of them is low then we can then either:

- decide on a solution from the data we have, or
- defer solving the problem to a later time, or
- decide not to solve it until it either occurs more often or has greater consequences.

The other part of the answer to the question 'how much data do we need?' will often, in the 'real' world, lie in the answers to:

- how much data do we have now?
- how much more data can we get and at what cost?

The scope and outcomes of problem data-gathering must reflect:

- the anticipated value of its outcomes
- the nature and accuracy of the input data.

But whatever the nature of our data we still need to solve our problems.

Logic or intuition

We don't always solve our problems in ways that are logical or rational. For example, we can 'jump' to a solution without evaluating any of the other possible solutions. Our choice of solution might be influenced by a number of factors such as personal preference and prejudice or the views of a strong leader or because this solution 'fits' with our long-term objectives. We can also arrive at a solution by intuition – without following any explicit or conscious logical train of thought. These and other similar processes are often referred to as 'creative' – rather than 'rational' – ways of solving our problems. They often seem unordered and complex. Nevertheless, they do represent powerful additions to the project manager's tool-box of problem solving techniques. We shall look at some of them in the following sections of this chapter. However, none of us can afford to throw rationality to the wind and this chapter will also look at a limited selection of numerical techniques for problem identification and solution. For more problem-solving techniques look in the books listed in the Further Information section at the end of the book.

A Nominal Group

This method of solving problems uses a group of people to find potential solutions to an identified problem. A very productive technique that can generate lots of good high quality ideas, it involves all the members of a group and uses consensus to evaluate and rank all the ideas generated. Its outcome is a group agreement about the action needed to solve a problem.

The steps are:

Step 1 The team leader presents the problem or opportunity to the group. This must be done in a way that does *not* suggest a preferred solution. The process and ground rules are also explained at this stage.

Step 2 Working on their own, everyone writes down a list of potential solutions for the stated problem.

Step 3 Everyone, in turn, reports a single idea. This is recorded on a flip chart or board. The name of the person who suggested the idea is not recorded, nor are any comments or evaluations made. This continues until all the ideas have been recorded.

Step 4 During a brief discussion any clarification of ideas needed is given and similar ideas are amalgamated – but only if the owners of the original ideas are agreeable.

Step 5 Each group member then identifies what she or he thinks are the 'top five' ideas of this composite list. She or he writes these down on a piece of paper and gives this to the leader – without sharing it with the group.

Step 6 The leader generates a top five list for the group from these lists.

Step 7 This is reported to the group and then discussed. Another vote taken to identify the idea(s) to be actioned

Most people find it difficult to report their ideas briefly and without commenting on their merits. The group leader must maintain the discipline of quickly moving on to the next person for each new idea. It is also important that the group stays together while the team leader – or someone else – is analyzing the options to find the group's top five.

Force Field analysis

It was an American social scientist called Kurt Lewin who first expressed the view that the ways in which people behave can be represented as a balancing act. What we balance are the opposing forces that act upon us. In any situation there are a number of these forces – some of these will seek to promote a change in our behaviour and others will seek to restrain or limit that change. This balancing act or equilibrium is not fixed or frozen, it is dynamic and interacts with the environment in which we work or play.

If we want to change this equilibrium situation then we must either weaken one or all of the restraining forces or strengthen one or all of the forces for change. The resulting imbalance will mean that a shift or change occurs and a new equilibrium is established. The forces can be anything that acts upon or is relevant to the situation.

Force field analysis can be used to solve our project problems. It is a simple, practical and proven way of deciding what you are going to do to solve your problem. You can use it on your own or in a team.

It has the following steps:

Step 1 Identify the problem and the desired outcome.

Step 2 Identify the forces involved – it may help if you classify them as either 'helping' or 'hindering' towards achieving the desired outcome.

Step 3 Decide which are the strongest 'hindering' and 'helping' forces.

Step 4 Decide whether you are going to:
- increase the 'helping' force, or
- eliminate or reduce the 'hindering' force.

Step 5 Develop action plans for the above.

Step 6 Implement the plans.

To work, this technique must have:

- a clear and unambiguous identification of the problem and the desired outcome
- a detailed and comprehensive identification of the forces
- a practical and realistic implementation plan.

This implementation can be seen as a sequence of three separate though connected stages:

- Unfreezing from current position
- Moving to new position
- Refreezing in new position.

Each of these stages must be carried through to completion. For example, let's assume that we have decided to solve our problem of inaccurate or out-of-date data for activity work rates by changing from a manual system to a new project management information system (PMIS). The first – and unfreezing – step would be to choose the new system and then tell everyone that we are going to introduce this. The movement step would involve the commissioning of the PMIS. The last – and refreezing – step in this simple example would be to ensure that all future client records were completed and stored on the new system. If any one of these stages was not completed then the solution to our problem would not work.

The Ishikawa diagram

Diagramming can often help us to solve our problems. The Ishikawa, 'Fishbone' or 'cause and effect' diagram is one of the most powerful of the problem solving diagramming techniques. Developed by Dr Kaoru Ishikawa, the diagram (see Figure 9.1) has, as its starting point, a box which is located on the right-hand side of a sheet of paper. The problem to be solved is written in this box and an arrow is then drawn across the sheet, pointing towards the box, and four further arrows are drawn pointing towards and joining the main arrow. Each of these side arrows represents a family or group of causes which could have lead to the problem. In its purest form the Fishbone diagram labels these side arrows with the tags of the 5Ms: Machinery, Manpower, Methods, Material and Maintenance. These can be extended to the 6Ms, by the addition of Mother Nature, or shrunk to the 4Ms by taking out Maintenance.

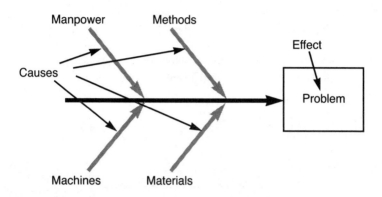

Figure 9.1 The Ishikawa or 'Fishbone' diagram with 4M headings

The technique can be used by a group or an individual and has the steps of:

Step 1 Clearly define the problem.

Step 2 Identify all possible causes, by brainstorming or by using the early steps of Nominal Group technique to generate lists of causes rather than solutions.

Step 3 Group the causes generated under the 4, 5 or 6M headings

Step 4 Visually connect all causes back to the problem using the Fishbone diagram. You may need to condense the cause descriptions at this stage.

Step 5 Use the diagram to continue the identification of possible causes until all of these, even the improbable ones, have been written down.

Step 6 Review the diagram and decide which of the causes are to be investigated first.

The diagram results in a thorough and often penetrating identification of all possible causes. It does not, of course, tell you which of those possible causes is the actual cause, but it does, if generated with care, give you confidence that all the possible causes have been listed. It is often worthwhile sticking to Ishikawa's original 5M headings in order to make sure that the review of causes is comprehensive and methodical.

Figure 9.2 shows how the technique could be applied – using the 4M headings – to one of the problems of the English Project that we met in Chapter 4.

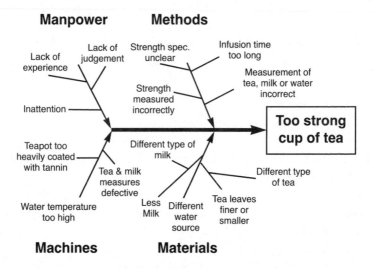

Figure 9.2   Example of the Fishbone diagram applied to a problem in the English Project

Pareto analysis

Most of our project problems have a range of possible causes. For example, our English Project tea can be too strong because the infusion time was too long or because the tea leaves were measured incorrectly or because we put in less milk than usual or because the tea leaves were old and dusty. If we have a repeated problem and if we've kept records of which of these causes seemed to apply, then we can use Pareto analysis to separate the major few from the many minor causes of our 'too strong' tea problem. Then we examine these major few further and develop action plans to eliminate them.

When Vilfredo Pareto studied the distribution of income in late 19th-century Italy, he found that around 90% of income went to about 10% of the population. He argued that this type of distribution is not just restricted to wealth or income but also occurs in many other situations. He then derived the Pareto principle. This tells us that, in general terms, the significant items in any group are in the minority – 'the vital few' – and the majority of the group are of relatively minor significance – 'the trivial many'. That is, that the minority of items in any group are the most significant in terms of their effect or consequences.

We can use Pareto analysis to identify the key causes of our project spend. as we saw in Chapter 8, and hence adjust our monitoring and reporting to reflect their importance. In our struggle to find solutions to our project problems, Pareto analysis can help us to identify those causes with either the highest frequency or the greatest consequence. In short, it enables us to focus our problem-solving efforts onto those key causes. As a result we should achieve maximum gain for minimum effort.

These are the steps:

Step 1 Assemble your data. Since we are considering each cause relative to the others, absolute accuracy is not that important. What is important is that the data for all the causes has the same level of accuracy and that this level of accuracy enables you to discriminate between the individual effects of the causes. At this time you will need some idea about the factor that will be used to contrast the effect of the individual items. This can be, for example, cost or frequency or consequence.

Step 2 Confirm that factor. It must be measurable but can also be generated by multiplying or adding or subtracting data for individual items. For example, the material usage costs can be generated by multiplying units used by unit cost. If it doesn't meet these criteria – then change it.

Step 3 Generate a table for the data in which you:

■ arrange it in descending order, i.e. with the largest figure at the top

■ generate the total for these figures

■ calculate the individual percentages of that total for each cause

■ calculate the cumulative percentage values.

Step 4 Identifying those items whose cumulative percentage lies below the 80% level in the above table. These are the 'vital few' and can be shown graphically by plotting these cumulative percentages against the cumulative number or percentage of items or by generating a bar chart (Figure 9.3) for individual percentage of total cost. It is these significant items that you will subject to more detailed analysis or monitoring. The object of that further analysis and monitoring is to identify and eliminate the causes of problems.

Figure 9.3   Bar chart of individual costs as percentage of total cost

Figure 9.4 is an example of how we can apply Pareto analysis to the problem of project material cost over-run. When we look at the Step 3 table and the bar chart in Figure 9.3 we can see that a minority of the items account for the majority of our project's total material spend.

PARETO ANALYSIS EXAMPLE

Step 1

Item	Unit price (£ per unit)	Usage (000s)
a	30	2.67
b	12	4.18
c	450	0.2
d	75	20
e	1500	0.5
f	800	7.0
g	200	6.0

Step 2

Item	Cost(£)
a	80,100
b	50,160
c	90,000
d	1,500,000
e	750,000
f	5,600,000
g	1,200,000

Step 3

Item	Cost (£)	% of Total Cost	Cumulative % of Total Cost
f	5,600,000	60.41	60.41
d	1,500,000	16.18	76.59
g	1,200,000	12.94	89.54
e	750,000	8.09	97.63
c	90,000	0.97	98.60
a	80,100	0.86	99.46
b	50,160	0.54	100.00
Total:	9,270,260		

Figure 9.4   Pareto analysis example

That is:

■ items f and d account for 76.59% of this total

■ items f, d and g account for 89.54% of this total.

These items' contribution to project material costs is between seven and nine times greater than that of the remaining items. This means that if we reduce spending on these items it will have a major effect on the project's total material spend.

From this simple example we can see that by using Pareto analysis, the project manager can identify those items that make a significant contribution to the project's costs. We can also see that Pareto analysis can tell us what we need to monitor frequently and, as importantly, what we do not.

CUSUM technique

The cumulative sum or CUSUM technique is used to detect changes in the trends of measured data. It can be used, for example, to monitor the ways in which achieved labour costs change or the ways in which achieved outputs such as bricks laid per day, or wall area painted per hour, change. One of its strengths is its ability to detect early shifts or movements in the data monitored.

The technique involves comparing the measured data to a previously established target and then plotting the cumulative sum of the differences.

The steps are:

Step 1 Establish a target for monitored factor. This can be a desired value or an historic average.

Step 2 Subtract the first measured data from this target. The difference can be negative or positive.

Step 3 Use this difference to begin to generate the cumulative sum of these differences

Step 4 Repeat Steps 2 and 3 for subsequent measured data and plot the value of the cumulative sum.

A simple example is shown in Figure 9.5 in which we can see that the slope of the CUSUM plot changes when the measured value changes. It does this in a way which is not damped by the 'smoothing' influence of any averaging process. This change tells us that something has happened and that 'something' may well require more detailed attention.

Week no.	Cable laid per day (x 100m)	Difference*	Cumulative Sum of Differences
1	6.2	– 0.2	– 0.2
2	6.7	+ 0.3	+ 0.1
3	6.9	+ 0.5	+ 0.6
4	5.9	– 0.5	+ 0.1
5	5.9	– 0.5	– 0.4
6	6.1	– 0.3	– 0.7
7	6.05	– 0.35	–1.05
8	6.2	– 0.2	–1.25

* Note: Target set at 640 metres per day

Figure 9.5a   CUSUM example

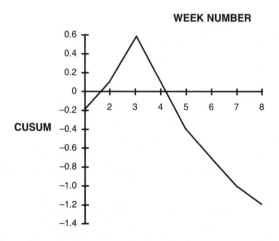

Figure 9.5b   Graph plotting the value of the cumulative sum of differences recorded in Figure 9.5a

Summary

The presence of problems on a project is not unusual. They occur, on almost a daily basis, in every project. They can be large or small, significant or inconsequential. Some of them have structure, certainty and clear alternative solutions whereas others display uncertainty, lack of structure and no clear alternatives. All of these problems have the potential to disrupt out project, and solving them is a key ability for the effective project manager. Most project problems arrive with limited data, no structure and no clear alternatives and the first step towards solving our problems lies in defining them – to a degree that reflects both their frequency and consequences and with amounts of data that reflect the anticipated value of project outcomes.

Problem solving isn't always a logical linear process and it can use a wide variety of techniques including Nominal Group technique, Force Field analysis, Ishikawa diagramming, Pareto and CUSUM analysis.

10 | CLOSING YOUR PROJECT

None of our projects lasts forever. They all – without exception – come to a close. The way in which that closure is conducted is just as important as the ways in which the project was planned, started, monitored and managed. This chapter looks at how we can close down our projects and examines the ways in which the close down of one project can contribute not only to its own success but also to the success of the next project.

Endings

The endings of our projects usually happen when the project outcomes are formally handed over. We saw in Chapter 1 that this marks the transition from the Production phase into the Termination phase in the project's life cycle.

But not all of our projects have such clean cut and obvious endings. For example, when the boundary between the project organization and the client organization is blurred or diffuse – as often happens in the integrated or the weak Matrix project organization (Chapter 3) – then the project outcome may not be the subject of a formal project team → client handover. It may have slipped gradually, almost imperceptibly, across the line between being a project outcome and becoming an organizational asset. When this happens the project outcome is gradually absorbed into the client organization as it grows and develops through the Production phase of its life cycle. Other projects collapse, fail or are terminated early. For these projects there is no project team → client handover to mark their end. They are abandoned. Their activity ceases, their failure becomes real. This can happen for a variety of reasons. The project's planned outcomes may have become obsolete or been superseded by alternatives developed elsewhere. Cheaper or faster or improved versions of its outcome may have hit the market place. Its prototypes may have failed to reach their hoped-for performance levels. The project costs or schedule may have run out of control. Its senior executive project champion may have fallen by the corporate wayside. All of these and other reasons can cause our projects to fail and when this happens they need to be closed down.

In all of these situations, whatever their point on the project life cycle, the project's activities – its **doing** – stop. Despite this apparent death, there is still work to be done, much of it about the fine detail of the project. The initial enthusiasm of the project's early days has passed; project team staff may be looking forward to returning to their pre-project duties or anticipating the challenge of the next project. Nevertheless this final stage of a project still represents a challenge to the effective project manager. In many ways, this challenge is greater than that of the earlier stages of the project's life cycle. This 'end-of-the-project' work also, surprisingly, possesses the potential to contribute to the success of the project.

Closure and the project manager

We already know that, to be competent and effective, the project manager must be able to lead, communicate, motivate and negotiate. In this, the closing phase of the project, the demand for these skills is just as high as it has been at any time of the project's life. The project manager has, for example, to lead and motivate a project team that is shrinking in size. The task of managing this shrinking team will not be made any easier by the fact that individuals left in this team may also be losing interest in the remaining tasks and showing reduced levels of motivation. They may even be concerned about their post-project futures.

The project manager also still faces the task of communicating with the projects' stakeholders. In the projects of our organizations the client's senior managers will be showing less interest in the project. Their attendance at project meetings will fall away, they will become less accessible than they were in the project's early stages. The level of interest of the organizations' operating staff will, however, be high. An all-consuming appetite for the details of the project outcome will have emerged.

In our homes, the project stakeholders will be just as involved or interested in the project outcome. The holiday in Hawaii will be in full swing, the sun-deck will have moved from pristine cleanliness to littered use, and the new car will have begun to lose that 'just-new' smell.

While all of this is happening, the business of project closure has to be carried out. The project manager will need, for example, to negotiate the completion of outstanding outcomes, contracts and work orders and the sale, disposal or storage of physical assets. She or he has to do so while the project team is shrinking and the stakeholder's acceptance of her or his authority is getting less. Small wonder then, that on large or complex projects, special project closure managers are appointed to ensure an orderly and effective end to the project.

But for all our projects – irrespective of their size, complexity or outcomes – all of these factors combine to create a unique and demanding set of problems which require management of a high order to ensure that the project is to be finally successful.

The closure process

When we close our projects we need to tidy up the loose ends. This means that we must ensure that all the project's work is done and its outcome is complete and available. It may mean that we need to make sure that all the project contracts are closed and all its equipment is sold off, relocated or mothballed. The project team members may need to be reassigned and the project's surplus materials disposed of. In short, we need to close the project's books.

All of this must be planned and budgeted in the same way as any other phase of the project. Abrupt and unplanned closure doesn't just leave too many loose ends and information gaps, it also leaves the client and other stakeholder's with diminished confidence in both the project team and the project outcome. However, we need to recognize that the inputs and outputs of this closure process are different from those of the more active and 'doing' phases of the project – as we can see in Figure 10.1.

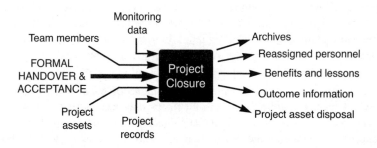

Figure 10.1   The project closure process

Earlier in this chapter we saw that the process of project closure can take place whether the project outcome is complete or not. We also saw that when closure is caused by project failure or early termination, there is no formal project team → client handover. But all the other elements of the project closure process remain. Project records need to be collated and stored, monitoring data archived, project assets disposed of or mothballed and team members relocated or reassigned.

If we fail to do all of this in an orderly and organized manner then not only do we leave behind the rubbish of our collapsed and incomplete intentions, but we also fail to learn from our mistakes and fail to grasp the benefits and lessons of managing our project.

Closing the team

A project is about people. This was so at its beginning and remains so through to its end. Throughout its life, these people are the project. As clients or customers, as members of a club or a family, even as the proverbial man or woman on the street, they are involved and interested. As project team members, their creativity, adaptability and energy plot, plan and manage the project's course. In this, the final project phase, the needs and concerns of these team members reach out beyond the now redundant boundaries of the project.

In the project teams of our organizations they become concerned with the answers to such questions as 'When will I leave this project team?' or 'Which project will I work on next?'or even 'Will I get my old job back?' These remaining team members will have seen the composition and size of the team change as people – usually key experts – move on to new projects. They may even have seen the project manager depart, leaving the job of 'tidying up the details' to a project team member who is less experienced or may have occupied a junior role on the team. In the projects of our homes and families the tidy, organized closure of our project inevitably slips down the priority lists of our busy lives.

All of this means that the ambitions and drive of the earlier, original, project team are gone. And with them, we may also have lost the co-operation and trust that carried the project to this, its completion. To manage this situation the project manager must make sure that both the project closure team and the client and other stakeholders refocus their earlier commitment to the project on to the task of project closure. The most effective way of doing this is by the use of joint teams; teams who are encouraged to self manage the definition and implementation of the remaining project tasks. For example, joint project team/client/stakeholder snag listing teams can audit the project outcome and identify a jointly agreed list of outstanding work or defects. The project manager and the project outcome's primary user can create joint plans for its transfer.

But, in the end, the project team must break up. Like all break ups, this needs to be managed with care. It needs to take into account the needs of both team members and the project. The project needs to maintain, even until its last 'gasp', an effective project team. The individual team members need to have their achievements recognized in one way or another. Time spent, by the project manager, in planning this team wind-down – even to the point of involving members of our organization's project teams in the creation of a reassignment plan – will pay dividends in terms of the commitment and performance of the remaining team members.

Closing the project data banks

By the time we reach this, the final stage of the project:

- almost all of the money will have been spent
- the project outcomes will have been created
- most of the project's resources will have been consumed.

A considerable amount of information will also have been created.

The nature of this information is various. It can include, for example, such things as:

- the drawings, technical specification and manuals of the equipment bought as part of the project
- the project outcome's technical or layout drawings
- the plans and programmes of project activities
- project spend records
- the contracts and subcontracts of the project.

The baseline of this information was contained in the project specification, the project plan and the project budget. Their contents will have been modified and extended by the actualities of the project's activities and the modifications created by project change control procedure.

So what are we going to do with all this information? The answer is that we need to use it to:

- identify and complete any outstanding work
- record the actual nature of the outcomes
- generate a project history
- check that we achieved what we set out to do.

When these are complete – and not before – we will be able to say that our project is complete.

Activity completion

The first step that we make towards our project completion enables us to find out what, if anything, is left to be done.

In order to do this we need to find out:

- what *has* been done
- what *ought* to have been done.

Not surprisingly, the difference between these will tell us if anything remains to be done.

Both of these have their roots and detail in documents such as the project specification, the project change control system and the Work Breakdown Schedule. With these as a starting point, joint project team/client/ stakeholder snag listing teams can audit the project. They can physically check what has actually been achieved and then compare this with what should have been achieved. The differences, if any, that exist between these tell us what is left to be done, if anything. They might even tell us that we have done more than was needed!

Finding out what is left to do is, initially, the more important. The client stakeholder needs to be sure that the project outcome is what he or she intended when the project was given its go-ahead. When differences appear between the project specification and the actual outcome then the project manager needs to agree, with all concerned, a programme for completion of this outstanding work. This programme should have agreed priorities and time scales and an outcome that completes the project specification. Until that is achieved the project manager's attention cannot move on towards an orderly and well managed closure of the project. On large projects this closure process can almost be a project in itself and for that reason can, as we saw earlier in this chapter, be managed by a close down or termination manager.

In Chapter 5 we saw the importance of effective communication to the project. This, the final stage of our project, is no exception to that rule. Indeed, it can be argued that the unique pressures and difficulties of this stage increase the need for effective communication. For example, the joint project team/client/stakeholder snag listing teams will generate information and feedback about what they find. These will be used to agree completion targets and the work undertaken towards those targets will need to be monitored and reported. Communication is always a two-way process and the project manager and client or stakeholder decision makers will need to have access to each other in order to ensure that briefing and debriefing occurs and that this, the final stage of the project, moves to an orderly conclusion.

The ways and means of this communication already exist. They are the project meetings and reports that, as we saw in Chapter 8, have been a regular and routine feature of the project's monitoring and control systems. During project closure it may be necessary to hold these meetings more frequently and to allow them to consider matters of detail – such as snag list team activities or work outstanding. The composition of the meeting will also change – now including all of the members of the smaller project team and client or stakeholder personnel involved in snag listing, commissioning, etc.

Project outcomes

Included in the information that is created by the project is information that is particular to the project's outcome.

For projects with tangible outcomes there are drawings or technical specifications. Purchased equipment will have operating manuals and warranties. Prototypes will have development logs and performance records. Our holiday project will have copies of booking forms and brochures. Even when the project outcome is low in tangibility this information still exists – as in the publicity material of political campaigns or the completed questionnaires of opinion surveys.

There should be little doubt about the need to transfer this material to the client.

For, in the future, it is the client, rather than the project manager, who will need to refer to or upgrade this information. If the project outcome is tangible, such as a new car or computer, it is the client – rather than project personnel – who will be responsible for its maintenance, repair or modification. Some of this information will be needed immediately after the formal hand-over to ensure that the client can start the operation and servicing of the project's outcomes. On projects with large and complex outcomes the hand-over of operating manuals may take place before the formal project outcome hand-over, in order to ensure that the client can plan and implement the training of operating personnel.

The collation and organization of all this documentation is not an end-of-project event. As we saw in Chapter 3, this documentation needs to be acquired, organized, collated and archived from the earliest days of the project. For example, purchase orders for equipment need to have clauses that ensure the provision of operating manuals, maintenance schedules, spares lists and trouble-shooting check lists. The delivery of this documentation needs to be progressed and quality controlled in the same way as the equipment itself.

There may also be circumstances in which the project team is involved in the start-up of the project outcome. This will occur when the outcome requires a particular expertise to ensure its efficient and effective start-up and operation. This, typically, is the sort of expertise that is difficult to acquire in any other than hands-on operation. On projects with large and complex outcomes, such as a chemical plant or an office block, the project start-up team is usually a stand-alone team that comes into existence at the late stages of the project's Production phase and may remain after the rest of the project team has left. On projects with small or less complex outcomes, such as a new personal computer or a car, the formal hand-over will include a user familiarization session.

Project histories

All projects have histories. These have their roots embedded in the project's records. They tell us of the project's life and times, remind us of the twists and turns of the changes in the project's plan, confirm the who-did-what-and-when of the project and tell us which procedures and systems were used. They chronicle the life and times of the project.

On big, complex projects with extended time scales, the project history can provide a valuable insight to the ways and means of project management. It can also, if generated as a rolling history – rather than an end-of-project retrospective – serve as a useful induction document for new project staff. For most projects, however, the generation of a full project history is a luxury. Its inevitable cost or the limited nature of the project doesn't warrant its generation. Under these circumstances, our retrospective view of the project is limited to that of the audit.

Project audits

An audit can be conducted at any point in the project's life. Its objectives are simple and straightforward and aims to identify:

- the project's current status
- the risks associated with that status
- whether we need to change the way the project is being managed or planned.

It is, however, unusual for audits to be conducted in the **doing** phases – the Planning and Design and the Production phases – of the project. When this does happen, it is usually because of massive delays or overspends – factors which have caused anxiety and concern amongst the project's stakeholders.

However, when we conduct a post-project audit, the project actions and activities have been completed and the project outcomes have been handed over to the client. As a consequence the objectives of the post-project audit are to identify things like whether any cost or plan overruns are justified and whether appropriate project management techniques were used. Obviously both the project manager and the client will have an interest in the outcomes of such an audit. Where both of these are employed by the same organization a single audit is not only sensible but also desirable. However, when the project manager/team is employed by a contractor then there may be value in an independent audit conducted by a third party.

The outcome of all post-project audits will be a formal report. The size, make-up and focus of this report will vary with the cost, nature and outcomes of the project. Large, expensive projects have audits which are conducted by a team of mixed disciplines and generate extended reports, usually to answer the needs of the organization's shareholders. The post-project audits of small or limited cost projects often consist of small reports. Reports on project outcomes with high levels of technical sophistication or those that require technical expertise – which the client may not possess – may be generated by independent technical experts.

However, these reports are not just book-keeping or cost accountancy exercises. They may, for example, reveal defects which are the subject of future legal action between a client, equipment suppliers or the project organization.

Post-project appraisals

Despite its investigative nature, the post-project audit does not tell us whether the project outcome has fulfilled its original promise and potential.

These, as we saw in Chapter 2, were an integral part of the information that we used to decide whether – or not – to spend the money required for the project's implementation. In Chapter 1 we saw that these outcomes can be concerned with any aspect of our lives – at work or at home. Their promises may have been about sales volumes and revenues, plant or equipment performance, reorganization, a new academic qualification, a new car or a holiday.

The post-project appraisal is about assessing whether what was promised was delivered and if not, why not. Without exception, it is initiated by the project client though it may be conducted, for reasons of impartiality or technical content, by a third party. In large organizations with many projects and high levels of capital expenditure, post-project appraisal is often conducted by a stand-alone department that is responsible to board level management. In our homes, our post-project appraisals are more informal in nature, often involving all who use or are involved in the project outcome. The post-project appraisals of the large projects of our organizations will review these projects from their conception through to two or three years after their completion. These reviews can take several months, involve a team of auditors and are presented in the form of a formal report.

As we saw earlier the post-project appraisal is – whatever the size or nature of the project outcome – primarily concerned with whether the project outcome has fulfilled its original promise and potential. But it can also be used as a 'where did we get it wrong' and 'where did we get it right' sort of exercise. From it we may learn to estimate our costs or evaluate our risks in different ways or to use different sorts of project planning tools. These lessons can be about details – as in 'next time we'll hire a bigger holiday car' – or about more fundamental issues – such as 'we'll never use that builder again'. All of these and other lessons come into being because of the post-project appraisal.

Summary

All projects come to an end. This happens either when they are formally handed over to a client or when they fail. In both of these situations the effective and efficient closure of a project still possesses the potential to make a contribution to the success of the project. This closure makes high demands upon the project manager's ability to lead, communicate, motivate and negotiate. These skills are used in a closure process whose prime objective is the orderly and organized completion and termination of not only the project but also its team, its data banks, its activities and the activities that lead to its outcome. The collation and archiving of the documentation associated with that outcome is also a part of that process as are the auditing of the project and the generation of its post-project appraisal.

11 | KEY ISSUES FOR PROJECT MANAGEMENT

This book has been a readable, practical and jargon-free introduction to the craft of Project Management. Its chapters have told you what is, and isn't, a project (Chapter 1); how to choose (Chapter 2), organize (Chapter 3), plan (Chapter 4), manage (Chapter 5) and monitor your project (Chapter 8) as well as how to assemble your project team (Chapter 6), manage your project money (Chapter 7), solve your project's problems (Chapter 9) and how to close your project (Chapter 10).

The objective of this, the final chapter of the book, is to summarize for you the key issues of project management. It also gives you – in the Project Manager Checklist (page 151) – the opportunity to test what you've learnt.

Key issues

Projects, projects and projects

- The project is a way of creating change.
- Its outcomes can be tangible or intangible.
- Projects can be large or small, involve any number of people and have life spans of days, years or decades.
- All projects have at their core the act of **Doing** – an act that is supported and reinforced by the acts of **Managing**, **Planning**, **Monitoring** and **Controlling**.
- The **Five Fundamentals** tell us that all projects:
  - are one-time efforts
  - are unique
  - have limited and defined times spans
  - are about change
  - have defined outcomes.

- The boundaries of the project have the dimensions of **Time**, **Cost** and **Performance**.
- Project life cycles have the phases of **Feasibility**, **Planning and Design**, **Production** and **Termination**.
- All project stakeholders need to be involved in the project's change process.

Which project?

- All projects involve risk and uncertainty.
- Using the two Cs – Cause and Consequence – we need to:
  - identify the type, level and source of that risk
  - reduce it
  - decide whether or not to accept it.
- Projects can be chosen by:
  - Non-numerical Methods to answer the demands of crises, legal requirements, employee welfare needs, individual's power or status needs, the organization's competitive needs and because they are 'nice to do'.
  - Numerical Methods such as Payback Period, Rate of Return, Net Present Value, Profitability Index and Internal Rate of Return.

Your project organization

- Projects need to be organized.
- The project organization needs to be compatible with the client organization.
- The project organization must provide a framework from within which the project's Doing, Planning, Monitoring and Controlling can be effectively carried out.
- Project organizations can be:
  - Integrated
  - Matrix
  - Stand Alone.
- You should seriously consider creating:
  - project manual
  - project specification

- change control procedure
- job descriptions
- responsibility charts
- budget and accounting procedures.

Plans for your project

■ The project plan converts project objectives into concrete realities.

■ To create a plan we need:
- the **what**, **when**, **who** and **with what** of the project's actions
- the project's budgeted cost.

■ The project plan can use:
- Gantt chart
- Activity on Arrow (AOA) network
- Activity on Node (AON) network.

■ Project's resources are planned and managed by either Resource Levelling or Heuristic rules.

Managing your project

■ Project management is different from day-to-day management.

■ The project manager is primarily concerned with creation of change using resources that are transient – rather than fixed, on a time scale that is frozen – rather than indefinite, to create a unique outcome – rather than a replication.

■ The project manager needs to be a gifted, broad view, generalist who can integrate or bring things together.

■ The effective project manager is able to:
- lead a team of skilled individuals
- communicate with all project stakeholders
- motivate the project team, contractors and sub-contractors
- negotiate effective solutions to the project's conflicts.

Your project team

■ Good project teams make things happen.

■ Team members have shared objectives.

- Team members are selected for:
  - a proven ability to work co-operatively
  - an ability to carry out the required team roles
  - their functional skills.
- Good teams rarely have more than ten members.
- Team building:
  - starts with a joint team charter
  - continues as the team spends time together
  - handles conflict constructively.
- Successful project team members:
  - have higher than average functional skills
  - are sensitive to the 'politics' of the project and its parent organization
  - have strong problem-solving skills
  - are willing to share both successes and mistakes.

Managing your project money

- An accurate estimate is vital to the success of a project.
- Generating an estimate is a logical exercise that is based on the available information about:
  - the project outcome
  - the project activities
  - information about the costs of identical or similar activities.
- The types of estimate are:
  - 'ball park', 'seat of the pants', 'order of magnitude' estimate (± 50%)
  - budget, predesign, feasibility estimate (±20%)
  - sanction estimate (± 10%)
  - definitive estimate (± 5–10%)
- These estimates can be:
  - top-down – using exponential or factorial estimating techniques, or
  - bottom-up – using costs generated from Work Breakdown Schedule (WBS) data.

■ 'Below-the-line' costs include:
- insurance
- tax charges
- allowances for inflation and contingencies.

■ The project estimate is the foundation of the project budget.

■ The project budget tells us what is to be spent and when it is to be spent.

Monitoring and controlling your project

■ Project monitoring and controlling are aimed at identifying and eliminating deviations from the project plan and budget.

■ Project monitoring involves:
- measuring
- recording
- collating
- analyzing.

■ The data used must be:
- relevant
- credible
- timely
- understandable
- connected to the project plan and budget.

■ Project monitoring can use project milestones, limit testing, the 80–20 rule, S curves, Earned Value Analysis and Critical Ratios.

■ Project control reduces the gap between what is actually happening and what we had planned should happen.

■ Project control is based on project monitoring.

■ Project control actions should be:
- appropriate
- quick
- cost effective
- reflect the size and nature of the difference.

Solving your project problems

- Problems occur, on almost a daily basis, in every project.
- All of these problems have the potential to disrupt our project.
- Most project problems arrive with limited data, no structure and no clear alternatives.
- Problem solving starts with problem definition.
- Problem solving isn't always a logical linear process.
- Problem solving can use a wide variety of techniques including Nominal Group Technique, Force Field analysis, Ishikawa diagramming, Pareto and CUSUM analysis.

Closing your project

- All projects come to an end – either when they are formally handed over or when they fail.
- The project closure process aims at the orderly and organized completion and termination of:
  - project
  - project team
  - project data banks
  - project activities.
- Project closure includes:
  - collation and archiving of the documentation
  - auditing of the project
  - the generation of post-project appraisal.

Conclusion

Managing a project is a demanding task – but one that can also be exhilarating and worthwhile!

The purpose of this book has been to make success in that task more accessible for all of you and to enable you to use the powerful tool of the project more effectively. But, in the end, the way that you manage your projects is up to you. It is truly an expression of your own individuality, rather than something brought down from some high mountain engraved on tablets of stone. My hope is that this book has enabled you to start to explore, change, refine and even reinvent the way you manage your projects.

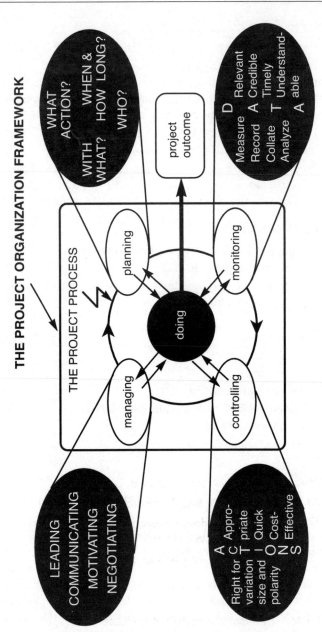

THE PROJECT ORGANIZATION FRAMEWORK

WHAT ACTION? WHEN & HOW LONG? WHO? WITH WHAT?

project outcome

D Measure Relevant
A Record Credible
T Collate Timely
A Analyze Understand-able

THE PROJECT PROCESS

planning

monitoring

doing

managing

controlling

LEADING
COMMUNICATING
MOTIVATING
NEGOTIATING

A Right for Appro-priate
C variation Quick
T size and Cost-
I polarity O Effective
N
S

Figure 11.1   The project process – the whole picture

PROJECT MANAGER
CHECKLIST

For each of the statements below, ring the number under the response which you feel is right for you when managing a project – and then add up your total.

	I agree	I agree most of the time	I'm not sure	I don't think I agree	No Way!
Monitoring is key to project success	1	2	3	4	5
A project team can make, or break, a project	1	2	3	4	5
If you listen to people, they listen to you	1	2	3	4	5
Plans provide a strong basis for management decisions	1	2	3	4	5
Change is an opportunity to be grasped	1	2	3	4	5
Conflict can be good if managed well	1	2	3	4	5

Key:

Total	
30–24	You can't be serious!
23–18	Some thought needed here.
17–12	Well done – a good score and a strong basis to build on.
12–6	Excellent – now go and do it.

Figure 11.2   Project manager checklist

GLOSSARY

Activity An element of project work, usually has a duration, cost, and resource needs.

Activity on Arrow or AOA network A project planning method that uses arrows to represent activities – also called Arrow Diagram Method (ADM).

Activity on Node or AON network A project planning method that uses nodes or boxes to represent activities – also called Precedence Diagramming Method (PDM).

Arrow Diagramming Method (ADM) see **Activity on Arrow**

ACWP Actual cost of work performed.

Bar chart see **Gantt chart**

BCWP Budgeted cost of work performed. Also called **Earned Value**.

BCWS Budgeted cost of work scheduled. Also called **Planned Value**.

Benefit Cost Ratio see **Profitability Index**

Budget A cost estimate for the project. The original cost estimate becomes the budget after sanction.

Cost Money given or surrendered in order to acquire, produce, accomplish, or maintain something; the price paid for something. (See also **Direct cost**, **Equipment cost**, **Fixed cost**, **Material cost**, **Labour cost**, **Indirect cost**, **Standard cost** and **Variable cost**)

Cost variance Difference between the estimated and the actual costs. In Earned Value Management expressed as (BCWP – ACWP).

Crashing Process of reducing project duration by analyzing alternatives for duration reduction at minimum cost.

Critical Activity Activity with zero or negative float, any activity on the Critical Path.

Critical Path   The sequence of activities which determines the earliest project completion.

Critical Ratio   An Earned Value Management ratio; (Actual Progress/ Scheduled Progress) × (Budgeted Cost/Actual Cost).

CPM   Critical Path Method, a network analysis technique used to find project duration by finding sequence of zero or least float activities. Also called Critical Path Analysis (CPA).

CUSUM   Cumulative Sum technique, a technique for trend detection.

Dependency   see Interdependency.

Direct costs   Costs which can be specifically identified with an activity.

Discounted Cash Flow (DCF)   see **Net Present Value**

Dummy   An activity in an AOA network which has zero duration but indicates interdependency.

Earned Value Analysis (EVA)   A project performance measurement method which compares planned and scheduled work. (Also see **ACWP**, **BCWS**, **BCWP**, **CV**, **SV** and **Critical Ratio**)

EET   Earliest Event Time, the earliest time by which an event can occur.

Equipment costs   Cost of lease, purchase, hire and use of equipment used in project.

Estimate   An approximate judgement, based on probability, of the cost or size of resources needed for a project task or activity.

Event   The beginning or end of an activity.

Five Fundamentals   All projects are one-time efforts, unique, about change and have limited and defined time spans and defined outcomes.

Fixed costs   Costs which remain at the same level irrespective of project workload.

Float   The amount of time that an activity can be delayed without delaying the project completion.

Gantt chart   A method of project planning. Activities are represented by horizontal bars whose length is proportional to the calendar time required for the activity.

Indirect costs   Costs not associated with an activity but associated with common objectives.

Integrated project organization   A type of project organization in which project activities are integrated into the structure of the client organization.

Interdependency   When an activity cannot be started until a prior activity or activities are complete.

Internal Rate of Return   The interest rate at which the project's Net Present Value is zero. (See **Net Present Value**)

Labour cost   Cost of employees

LET   Latest event time, the latest time by which an event can occur.

Material cost   Cost of materials and other commodities

Matrix organization   A project organization in which the project manager shares control of and responsibility for team members with their functional boss.

Milestones   Significant points in a project, usually events on the Critical Path.

Monitoring   The acquisition, collation, analysis and reporting of data about project performance.

Net Present Value or NPV   The algebraic sum of the capital required to implement the project and the present values of the estimated future profits for defined number of years.

Node   A point of connection in a project planning network, the beginning or end of an activity in an AOA network, the activity itself in an AON network.

Nominal Group Technique   Problem solving technique.

Overheads   see **Indirect costs**

Parallel activities   Activities which can be done at the same time.

Parametric estimating   An estimating technique that uses historical cost data and relates it to outcome characteristics such as square footage, output, lines of software, etc.

Pareto principle   A relationship that tells us that the significant items in any group are in the minority – 'the vital few' – and the majority of the group are of relatively minor significance – 'the trivial many'. That is that the minority of items in any group are the most significant in terms of their effect or consequences.

Payback period The period of time taken for the project's cumulative cash flow to reach zero.

PERT Programme Evaluation and Review Technique – a network analysis technique used to estimate project duration when there is uncertainty about activity durations

Precedence Diagramming Method (PDM) see **Activity on Node**

Profitability Index The ratio of the NPV of the project to the capital required.

Project A sequence of connected events that are conducted over a defined and limited period of time and are targeted towards generating a unique but well defined outcome.

Project key dimensions Cost, Time and Performance.

Project life cycle Feasibility, Planning and Design, Production, Termination.

Project specification The definitive source of information about a project's scope, goals and objectives, organization, budget and justification.

Rate of return Annual profit/implementation cost $\times$ 100%.

Ranking A method of choosing between alternative projects by generating the sum of each alternative's rankings, relative to each other, under a number of criteria.

Resource Something that is needed in order to do work – money, equipment, people, information, skill, knowledge, materials.

Resource levelling Smoothing of resource usage patterns.

Risk The estimated degree of uncertainty.

Schedule variance The difference between the scheduled and actual completion levels. In Earned Value Management expressed as (BCWP – BCWS).

Slack see **Float**

Stand-alone project organization A type of project organization in which the project team exists as a stand-alone organization – separate from the client organization.

Stakeholders People or organizations with something to gain or lose by the way the project turns out.

Standard costs   Calculated costs, often historic, which are used in both project estimating and monitoring.

Uncertainty   The lack of information about the duration, occurrence or value of future events.

Variable costs   Costs which vary with the rate of project workload or activity.

Variance   The difference between what has been estimated or budgeted and what has been achieved. (See **Cost Variance** and **Schedule Variance**)

Work Breakdown Schedule (WBS)   A structured list of project activities and tasks with descending level giving more detail.

Zero Float   Condition which occurs when there is no excess or spare time between activities. (See **Critical Activity**)

FURTHER INFORMATION

Books

Project management is a growing field and there are always new books being published. This list is intended to start you off on further reading. To browse for (or buy) other books try The Bookstore on the PMI web site, or the Amazon, Blackwells or Borders web sites.

General

Cleland, D.I. (ed.), *Field Guide to Project Management*, 1997, Wiley.

Dinsmore, P. (ed.), *AMA Handbook of Project Management*, 1993, AMACOM.

Lock, D., *Project Management*, 6th Edn, 1996, Gower.

Meredith, J.R. and Mantel, S.J., *Project Management – a managerial approach*, 3rd Edn, 1995, Wiley.

Planning

Lockyer, K.G. and Gordon, J., *Critical Path Analysis and Other Project Network Techniques*, 1995, Pitman.

Mulvaney, J., *Analysis Bar Charting*, 1980, Management Planning & Control Systems.

Sectors

Badiru, A.B., *Project Management for Research*, 1995, Chapman & Hall.

Black, K., *Project Management for Library and Information Service Professionals*, 1996, Aslib.

Cotterell, M. and Hughes, R., *Software Project Management*, 1995, ITP New Media.

Greasley, A., *Project Management for Product and Service Improvement*, 1998, Butterworth-Heinnemann.

Roberts, K. and Ludvigsen, C., *Project Management for Health Care Professionals*, 1998, Butterworth-Heinemann.

Smith, N., *Engineering Project Management*, 1995, Blackwell.

Whitaker, R., *Project Management in the Process Industries*, 1995, Wiley.

Woodward, J., *Construction Project Management*, 1997, Am. Soc. Civil Eng.

Yeates, D., *Project Management for Information Systems*, 1996, Financial Times.

Analytical methods

Anderson, D., Sweeney, D.J. and Williams, T., *Quantitative Methods for Business*, 7th edn, 1997, South Western.

Fleming, Q.N. and Koppelman, J.M., *Earned Value Project Management*, 1996, Project Management Institute.

Communication

Baguley, P., *Effective Communication for Modern Business,* 1994, McGraw-Hill, Maidenhead.

Heller, R., *Communicate Clearly*, 1998, Dorling Kindersley.

3M Meeting Management Team, *How to Run Better Business Meetings*, 1987, McGraw-Hill.

Organizations

Morgan, G., *Imaginization: The Art of Creative Management*, 1993, Sage.

Pedler, M., Burgoyne, J. and Boydell, T., *The Learning Company*, 1991, McGraw-Hill.

Problem solving

de Bono, E., *Lateral Thinking for Management*, 1990, Penguin.

Henry, J. (ed.), *Creative Management,* 1991, Sage, London.

Weiss, D.H., *Creative Problem Solving*, 1988, AMACOM.

Teams

Belbin, M.R., *Management Teams*, 1996, Butterworth-Heinemann.

Belbin M.R., *Team Roles at Work*, 1996, Butterworth-Heinemann.

Katzenbach, J.R. and Smith D.K., *The Wisdom of Teams*, 1992, Harvard Business School Press.

Professional associations

Australia

Australian Institute of Project Management
PO Box 420
Spit Junction
NSW 2088
Australia
Tel: +2 9960 0058
Fax: +2 9960 0052

France

Association Francophone de Management de Projet
3 Rue Française
75001 Paris
France
Tel: + 1 42 36 36 37
Fax: + 1 42 36 36 35

South Africa

Project Management Institute of South Africa
PO Box 68858
Bryanston 2021
South Africa
Tel and Fax: +27 11 4631022

United Kingdom

Association for Project Management
85 Oxford Road
High Wycombe
Bucks HP11 2DX
England
Tel: + 44 14 94 44 00 90
Fax: + 44 14 94 52 89 37
e-mail: secretariat@apm-uk.demon.co.uk

United States

Project Management Institute
Four Campus Boulevard
Newton Square
Pennsylvania 19073-3299
USA
Tel: 610 – 356 – 4600
Fax: 610 -356 – 4647
e-mail: pmihq@pmi.org

PMI has 'chapters' in 45 countries including Australia, Belgium, Canada, Chile, Egypt, France, Germany, India, Indonesia, Israel, Italy, Japan, Luxembourg, Malaysia, Mexico, Netherlands, New Zealand, Philippines, Russia, Saudi Arabia and South Africa. For access information write to above or access web site at www.pmi.org

International

International Project Management Association
PO Box 30
Monmouthshire NP5 4YZ
United Kingdom
Tel: + 44 1594 531007
Fax: + 44 1594 531008
e-mail: ipma@btinternet.com

IPMA has national associations in Austria, China, Czech Republic, Denmark, Egypt, Finland, France, Germany, Greece, Hungary, Iceland, India, Ireland, Italy, Republic of Macedonia, Netherlands, Norway, Portugal, Russia, Slovakia, Slovenia, Spain, Sweden, Switzerland, Ukraine, UK and Yugoslavia. For access information write to above or access web site at www.ipma.ch

Some useful web sites

Web sites are notoriously fickle creatures – here today, gone tomorrow.
Try these:

msfcdb2.msfc.nasa.gov/evm – NASA Earned Value page with links

www.acq.osd.mil/pm – Earned Value site with links and software tools
pages

www.afitep.fr/main.html – Association Francophone de Management de
Projet site

www.amazon.com or www.amazon.co.uk – The biggest Web bookshop

www.apm.org.uk – Association for Project Management site

www.blackwells.co.uk – Blackwells bookshop

www.borders.com – Borders bookshop

www.bsi.org.uk – British Standards Institution site – check on BS 6079,
BS 6046 and BS ISO 10006

www.ccta.gov.uk – Link to Official PRINCE2 home page

www.concentric.net/~Yarrainc/yarra7.htm – A humourous look at 'The
Laws of Project Management'

www.dab.uts.edu.au – Project management page has link to Australian
Institute of Project Management site

www.fek.umu.se/irnop/projweb – This is the 'WWW Guide to Project
Management Research Sites 'and is maintained by Umeå School of
Business and Economics, Sweden – lots of useful links.

www.hotbot.com – Said by many to be the best search engine.

www.icoste.org – International Cost Engineering Council site – link page
to member associations

www.ipma.ch – International Project Management Association site

www.nssn.org – American National Standards Institution search site for
international standards

www.pmforum.org – A Canadian site rich in PM information

www.pmi.org – Project Management Institute site – contains on-line 'Project
Management Body of Knowledge', PMI Bookstore and Links page

www.project-manager.com – Worth a visit

www.wst.com – A commercial site which has an extensive glossary of
project management terms in its library section.

INDEX

ABC analysis 110
Abraham Maslow 75
above-the-line costs 100
activity 152
   dummy 58–60, 153
   interdependency 50–2, 154
   on arrow network 56–60, 64, 146, 152
   on node network 56, 64, 146, 152
   parallel 50, 53, 154
   slack 59, 61, 155
ACWP 112, 152
agendas 114
Akashi–Kaikyo bridge 4
allowances 101, 103, 148
   contingency 101, 103
   inflation 101, 103
American Institute of Architects (AIA)
   41
American National Standards
   Institute (ANSI) 41, 161
Avebury stone circle 3

balancing act 123
ball park estimate 94, 103, 147
bar charts 52–5, 152
bargaining 73
   zone 75
BCWP 112, 152
BCWS 112, 152
below-the-line costs 101, 103, 148
benefit cost ratio 28, 152
bottom-up estimates 99, 103, 147
British Standards 41, 161
budgets 43, 45, 101, 103, 148, 152
budget estimate 103

Cause and Consequence 19, 29, 145
cause and effect diagram 124

change control 43, 45, 117, 145
choosing 17–29
   by numbers 26–8, 145
   without numbers 23–6, 145
check lists
   project team 89
   project manager 151
closure 133–43, 149
Colossus of Rhodes 3
Coliseum of Rome 3
communication
   and project closure 139
   and project managers 71–2, 77
computers
   software 63, 64
   in planning 62
contingency allowance 101, 103
controlling 115–17, 118, 148
conflict
   stakeholder 16
   team 86, 147
cost 11, 16, 92, 112, 145, 147, 152
   above-the-line 100
   below-the-line 101
   control 110, 115
   estimates – see estimates
   monitoring 111
   types 92, 153, 154, 156
   variance 113, 119, 152, 156
CPA or CPM 56, 153
critical path 53, 54, 59, 62, 153
critical ratio 113, 118, 119, 148, 153
CUSUM technique 130, 132, 149, 153

decisions 82
definition of project 10–11
definitive estimate 95, 103
design and planning phase 13, 16, 155

direct costs 93, 153
discounted cash flow 27, 153
dummy activity 58, 153
duration 49, 50, 51, 54

Earned Value analysis 112–14, 118,
    148, 153
EET 58–9, 153
English Project 49–52, 53, 55
equilibrium 123
estimate 92–101, 147, 153
    accuracy 94–5, 103
    data sources 95–7
    types 94–5, 103, 147
estimation methods
    exponential 98, 147
    factorial or parametric 98, 147
    activity based method 98
events 56–9, 153
    earliest time 58, 153
    latest time 58, 153

factorial estimating 98
feasibility phase 13, 16, 94, 145, 155
Fishbone diagram 124–6
Five Fundamentals 8–10, 16, 144, 153
fixed costs 93, 153
float 59, 153
Force Field analysis 123, 132, 149

Gantt charts 52–5, 63, 64, 108, 146, 153
GERT 56
Great Wall of China 3

heuristics 62, 64, 146
Hong Kong – Chek Lap Kok
        airport 4

indirect costs 93, 153
inflation 101, 103
influencing projects 7
information 30, 95, 135, 147, 157
integrated project organization 36, 45,
    145, 154
interdependency 50–2, 154
internal rate of return 28, 145, 154
Ishikawa diagram 124–6, 132, 149

job descriptions 42, 45

key dimensions 12, 145

labour costs 93, 110, 112, 154
leadership 68–71, 77, 146
life cycle 13–15, 16, 145, 155
limit testing 109, 118
LET 58–60, 154

managers 65–8, 69, 77
management 65, 77
managing projects 1, 6, 66–8
material costs 93, 110, 154
matrix project organization 38, 40, 45,
    145
Mayan temples 3
meetings 72, 114, 139
    chair people 115
milestones 109, 118, 148, 154
money 92
monitoring 105–15, 117, 148, 154
    A,B &C 110
    and project budget 111
    and project plan 108
    earned value 112
    limit testing 109
    milestones 109
    pulse points 107
    reports and meetings 114
motivation
    Abraham Maslow 75
    and project managers 75–7, 146

NASA
    lunar landing 4
    Mars project 6
    saying 88
negotiating 72–5, 77, 146
    and bargaining 73
    ways and means 74
net present value 27, 29, 145, 154
networks 56–60
    AOA or ADM 56, 63
    AON or PDM 56, 63
node 56, 58, 154
Nominal Group 122–3, 132, 149

organizations 31
  and projects 33
  project 34, 36–41, 145
  structure, leaders and people 32
outcomes 4, 6, 7, 8, 9, 10, 14, 16, 143
overheads 93

parametric estimating 98, 147
Pareto analysis 110, 126–30, 132, 149,
  154
payback period 26, 29, 145
PERT 56
people
  and organizations 32
  and projects 15
  and project closure 136
Pharos of Alexandria 3
plan
  monitoring 108
  types 52–60
planning 5, 46–64, 146
planning and design phase 13–14
precedence networks 56, 155
preliminary estimate 95
PRINCE 41
problems 119–21, 149
problem solving 122–32, 149
problem solving techniques
  Nominal Group 122, 149
  Force Field analysis 123, 149
  Ishikawa diagram 124, 149
  Pareto analysis 126, 149
  CUSUM technique 130, 149
production phase 14, 16, 145
profitability index 28, 29, 145
PROMPT 41
post project
  appraisals 142, 143, 149
  audits 141, 143, 149
progress reports 114, 118
project
  appraisal 142, 143, 149
  audits 141, 143, 149
  budgets 43, 45, 101, 103, 148, 152
  boundaries 11
  change control 43, 45, 117, 145

choice 17–29
choice by numbers 26–8, 145
choice without numbers 23, 26, 145
closure 133–43, 149
communications 71–2, 77, 139
conflict 16, 86, 147
control 110, 115, 118, 148
critical path 53, 54, 59, 62, 153
cost 11, 16, 92, 112, 145, 147, 152
definition 10–11
duration 49, 50, 51, 54
English 40–52, 53, 55
estimates and budgets 92–103
Five Fundamentals 8–10, 16, 144,
  153
home 3, 4, 6, 7, 11
inputs 30
individual 7
influencing 7
key dimensions 12, 45
life cycle 13–15, 16, 145, 155
management 65–7
manual 41, 145
milestones 109, 118, 148, 154
monitoring 105–15, 117, 148, 154
organization 33–41
outcomes 4–7, 9–16, 20, 34–6, 95,
  103, 107, 116, 135, 139, 144,
  147, 150
performance 12, 15, 16, 106, 155
plans 46–64, 146
problems 119–21, 149
procedures and specifications 41–4
priorities 15
resources 61
roles and responsibilities 42
specification 42, 45, 145
team 78–91, 146
project manager 65–77
  check list 151
project managers and communication
  71, 146
  leadership 68, 146
  motivation 75, 146
  negotiation 72, 146

projects
   and change 4, 9, 16, 144
   and day-to-day activities 66
   and doing 4, 5, 16, 144
   and managing 5, 16, 144
   and people 9, 30, 136
Pyramid of Giza 3

ranking 25, 29, 155
rate of return 27, 29, 155
   internal 28, 29
reports 72, 114
resources 30, 61, 155
resource levelling 61, 64, 146, 155
responsibility chart 44, 45, 146
risk 18–21, 145
   identification 19
   reduction 20
risk matrix 20

S curve 111, 118, 148
sanction estimate 95, 103, 147
schedule variance 113, 155
selecting your project 17–29
   organization 39
specification 42, 45, 145
   project
slack – *see* float
stakeholders 15, 16, 35, 65, 68, 71, 77,
   114, 118, 134, 139, 143, 145

stand-alone project organization 93, 156
standard costs 93, 156
Sydney Opera House 4
teams 78–91, 146
   and groups 79
   bad teams, good teams 80
   building 85
   charter 84
   check list 89–90
   members 82
   size 81
termination phase 14, 16, 145, 155
top-down estimate 97, 103, 147
Toronto, CN tower 4

uncertainty 18, 19, 156

variable costs 93, 156
variance 156
   cost 113, 119, 152, 156
   schedule 113, 119, 155
VERT 56
Vilfredo Pareto 10, 127

work breakdown schedule (WBS) 50,
   96, 103, 156

Xiaolangdi dam 4

Other related titles

ty TEACH YOURSELF

BUSINESS PRESENTATIONS

Angela Murray

Giving a presentation can be a daunting and nerve-racking experience, even for a regular presenter – what can you do to give yourself confidence and ensure success? *Teach Yourself Business Presentations* provides the answer. From defining the brief to post-presentation analysis, the book supplies a step-by-step guide to the skills and techniques needed to deliver an effective, engaging presentation.

Team presentations, presentations to colleagues, informative and persuasive presentations – appropriate techniques are considered for these and many more. Throughout the book imagination, innovation and creativity are all actively encouraged.

Covered in the book:

- strategic planning – defining and analyzing the brief
- planning and research
- creativity
- communication skills
- audio-visual aids
- 'presentation etiquette' and personal presentation
- analyzing performance.

An easy-to-read guide, full of hints and tips, this book provides support and guidance for the novice, and fresh ideas for the more experienced.

Angela Murray is a freelance Business Consultant specializing in marketing communications and presentation skills.

Other related titles

TEACH YOURSELF

PERFORMANCE APPRAISALS

Polly Bird

All managers have to carry out staff appraisals, and *Teach Yourself Performance Appraisals* provides the guidelines and help on how to do this effectively and obtain the desired results. The book deals with each stage of appraising, from preparation to evaluation. It also gives advice on how to cope with difficulties during the appraisal process, as well as how to handle your own appraisal.

The book is written in a practical and straightforward way and includes:

- guidance to managers new to appraisals, and those who want to improve
- advice on how to turn discussion into action
- help with upward appraisals.

Polly Bird is a professional writer of business and training books.

ty TEACH YOURSELF

IMAGINATIVE MARKETING

J Jonathan Gabay

Powerful marketing campaigns are based on original thinking and creative planning. *Teach Yourself Imaginative Marketing* concentrates on the engine which drives successful marketing – imagination. Revealing many profitable tips and secrets to help you target, brand and sell your enterprise whilst generating provocative publicity, this book will keep you three steps ahead of the competition.

The book:

- covers the key marketing areas of sales, advertising, PR and branding
- concentrates on the dynamic 'imaginative' side of marketing
- is easy to follow with useful activities and exercises
- includes a comprehensive 'jargon buster' section
- is suitable for anyone working in or studying marketing.

Completely up-to-date, ready for the cut-and-thrust world of marketing beyond the millennium, this book is indispensable for anyone who wants their business and careers to succeed and continue to breed success.

J Jonathan Gabay, a Course Director at the Chartered Institute of Marketing, has worked for some of the world's biggest advertising agencies and on some of the best-known marketing brands.